Gaudí

Gaudí

John Gill

p

This is a Parragon Publishing Book
This edition published in 2004

Parragon Publishing
Queen Street House
4 Queen Street
Bath BA1 1HE, UK

Copyright © Parragon 2001

ISBN: 1-40542-976-3

Picture research: Image Select International

Printed and bound in China

GAUDÍ CHRONOLOGY

1878–2	Works in Parc de la Ciutadella
1878–89	Lampposts, Plaça Reial and Barceloneta
1881	Mataró Workers' Cooperative
1883–5	Casa Vicens
1883–5	Villa Quijana (El Capricho)
1884–7	Pavilions Güell
1886–9	Palau Güell
1887–93	Palacio de Astorga
1889–94	Colegio de Santa Teresa de Jesús
1892–3	Spanish Franciscan mission, Tangier
1892–4	Casa de Los Botines, León
1895–1901	Bodegas Güell
1898–1904	Casa Calvet
1898–1914	Crypt of the Colonia Güell church
1889–1914	Palma de Mallorca cathedral
1900–14	Park Güell
1900–2	Torre Bellesguard
1901–2	Finca Miralles
1904–6	Casa Batlló
1906–12	Casa Milà (La Pedrera)
1908	New York Hotel
1883–1926	Sagrada Familia

CONTENTS

Contents

INTRODUCTION

ANTONI Gaudí i Cornet—to give him his full name, following the Spanish tradition of adopting paternal and maternal surnames—was only one of the young architects whose buildings made Barcelona world famous in the late nineteenth and early twentieth centuries. He was, however, the only one who invented a radical new language for architecture, fusing traditional and seemingly avant-garde ideas into a hybrid form that stunned observers. His greatest works, such as the temple of the Sagrada Familia, approach the mystical and involve feats of engineering and imagination that verge on, perhaps enter into, the sublime. Gaudí can also be said to have invented a new, popular form of ecclesiastical architecture, explicitly designed to bring the ordinary person closer to God.

If Gaudí is seen as the chief agent in transforming *fin del siglo* Barcelona, he was also utterly a product of the city, the region, and his era. Born in Riudoms in the countryside outside Tarragona in 1852, educated in the nearby city of Reus, and trained in Barcelona, he lived through one of the most turbulent periods in Spanish history. Throughout the nineteenth century and up to the start of the Civil War in 1936, Spain was riven by anticlerical uprisings, right-wing conspiracies, military coups, and anarchist violence. Barcelona, its most industrialized city, became a focus for these forces. Its economy was volatile, swinging from boom to bust and back again. As the capital of Catalonia, Barcelona was also the natural center for a powerful Catalan regionalist culture, one that traced its heritage back to the troubadour poets of the Middle Ages, and which promoted an aggressive linguistic, cultural, and political separatism from the rest of Spain that still simmers today. All of these forces would influence and even be described in Gaudí's work.

The young Gaudí did not seem destined for greatness, less still the extraordinary campaign for his beatification, or elevation to sainthood, currently working its way through the corridors of the Vatican. Born into a family of artisan metalworkers, he was a sickly child, troubled by rheumatism from an early age. He was an average school pupil, but his poor health seems to have left him time to study the larger world around him. Only at fourteen, when he began to excel in geometry, a skill he later attributed to his relatives' work in three-dimensional metal structures, did his talents declare themselves. He started contributing illustrations to a school magazine, and designed sets for school drama productions. He also began hiking with friends, often visiting ruined Gothic sites such as the nearby monastery at Poblet, and at the age of fifteen he and two friends hatched the farseeing (if unrealized) project of restoring Poblet and opening it to tourists to fund the restoration.

As he would later say, "A deep-seated preoccupation drove me to dwell on the stability of buildings." He moved to Barcelona at sixteen to finish his schooling, and began to prepare for studies as an architect. Here too he was an undistinguished student, although perhaps Barcelona's School of Architecture wasn't capable of drawing out his talents. Set an exercise to design a cemetery gate, Gaudí, perhaps laterally-minded, said he had to draw the road to the cemetery and the mourners before attempting the gate. They flunked him.

Gaudí worked as an assistant in the offices of architect Josep Fontseré i Mestres to support his studies. Fontseré had been commissioned to design the city's new Parc de la Ciutadella, and the young Gaudí's hand has been detected in some of its features. One contribution is unquestioned: Gaudí realized that the plans for the tank feeding the Parc's monumental fountain were dangerously flawed, and offered Fontseré an alternative design which his employer gratefully accepted. This precocious achievement won Gaudí a pass mark when news of it reached his hitherto unimpressed architecture professors.

If Gaudí had an intellectual hero it was the French medievalist Viollet-le-Duc. Gaudí was particularly struck by Viollet-le-Duc's insistence that the past isn't there to be imitated but to be built on. This sense of doing something new or different with a given style or material would inform Gaudí's work throughout his career. Outside the School of Architecture curriculum, he read extensively in history, politics, and economics, to better understand how social factors change the shapes of buildings. He also devoted himself to the study of ancient monumental architecture, a study that would literally underpin his greatest works.

His first commission was for a workers' cooperative center south of Barcelona, which might suggest an interest in the embryonic socialist movement. If that was the case, Gaudí was swiftly disabused of any socialist leanings: with the exception of his ecclesiastical buildings, he would spend the rest of his career designing trophy homes for the fabulously wealthy new rich of Barcelona's industrial boom. Their patronage would also steer him into the charmed and possibly masonic circles of patrician Catholic conservatives. Patronage and friendship won him prestigious commissions, including, at the age of 32, El Templo Expiatorio de la Sagrada Familia, the Expiatory (i.e., penitential) Church of the Sacred Family.

Gaudí worked on the Sagrada Familia until three days before his death in 1926, although he only saw one of its twelve towers, that of St Barnabas, finished. His work was continued by assistants and, later, outside architects commissioned by the private foundation that oversees the Sagrada Familia. Debate continues over whether it should be left as it was when Gaudí died or if it should be completed. Controversy still surrounds modern interpretations of Gaudí's drawings for the building: notoriously, he worked from sketches that he frequently altered, and left no fixed, final plans for the Sagrada. It remains unfinished to this day, although work continues almost every day of the year.

The commission that launched Gaudí's career was a small but exquisitely worked display case that found its way to the Paris Exposition in 1878 and to the attention of Eusebi Güell i Bacigalupi. Güell, heir to

one of Barcelona's wealthiest business families, sought out the designer on his return home. They became firm friends, and Güell would be Gaudí's chief patron until his death.

Gaudí's early buildings displayed certain echoes of Mudéjar, the Spanish–Arabic style inspired by Spain's Moorish past, and Gothic, but from the first private commission, Casa Vicens, it was clear that these were, to borrow a line from a Talking Heads song, "houses in motion." Gaudí was already pushing engineering and design beyond their limits, often to the alarm of his workmen, who feared his buildings would collapse (they didn't). His great secular buildings, such as the Casa Batlló and Casa Milà, cut the moorings of conventional architecture entirely and assumed fluid, organic, animal, and even human forms. In the Sagrada Familia, he marshaled these techniques in a "cathedral" that was simultaneously breathtaking and kitsch and which, for an "expiatory" building, atoning for the sins of modern civilization, manages also to be unequivocally arrogant in its ambition and hubris. These are by no means the only contradictions in the work of Antoni Gaudí i Cornet.

Gaudí's work coincided with the explosion of *modernisme* in Barcelona, a movement inspired and bankrolled by Barcelona's industrial boom. However, it remains largely that; a coincidence. Where the *modernistas* took their cue from French art nouveau and German *Jugendstil*, Gaudí was heading in the opposite direction. Some of the great *modernista* buildings, such as Lluís Domènech i Montaner's dazzling Palau de la Música Catalana, are as impressive as any of Gaudí's secular buildings, but Gaudí had an entirely different agenda. He despised modernism, although it is clear that he took ideas from it to use to his own ends. Those ends were the search for pure form, a search that took him back to the tree and the bone. He was also looking for an architecture that would glorify Catalonia, hence the dense and often ambiguous symbolism in his work. In his ecclesiastical work, such as the Sagrada Familia and the renovation of the cathedral in Palma de

Mallorca, he wanted to improve on the flaws of Gothic architecture—he abhorred flying buttresses, for example, calling them "crutches"—and to seat the congregation, literally and metaphorically, closer to their God.

His private life remains an enigma; it is entirely possible that he poured his life, certainly the last decades of it, into his work. He never married, despite a number of inconclusive romances, and it appears that he experienced a crisis in middle age, one that pushed him deeper into obsessive religiosity. (This is the motor that drives the current campaign for his beatification.) A dandy about town in his youth, he later adopted an ascetic lifestyle, fasting, giving away his belongings, finally, as the Sagrada Familia stumbled from financial crisis to financial crisis, begging for money to continue the project. In his last years, he became a hermit, sleeping in his office, eating little, attending mass daily. It is possible that his punishing lifestyle fed his mystical vision. He told one friend: "As I feel my body growing weaker, I feel my spirit growing more agile." He told another concerned visitor: "I am not alone. I am surrounded by an endless array of marvels."

When he was run over by a tram in June 1926, to die of his injuries three days later, the 72-year-old Gaudí looked so ragged he was taken to a paupers' hospital. When his friends found him, he refused to be moved to another hospital. Yet after his death Gaudí's body "lay in state," and thousands turned out for his funeral.

With the passing of *modernisme*, his work fell out of critical favor, and was dismissed as eccentric, almost vulgar. Yet Le Corbusier and, a little belatedly, Nikolaus Pevsner, championed him. Salvador Dalí claimed him for the surrealists—something that would surely have made the deeply conservative Gaudí spin in his grave—and the teenage Joan Miró adored the mosaics in Gaudí's unfinished Park Güell. In his monumental *Barcelona*, critic Robert Hughes writes that in the 1960s hippies would smoke dope to better appreciate the fantastical Park Güell or the Sagrada Familia (one imagines the rotating señor Gaudí picking up speed in his

coffin down there in the Sagrada crypt). Yet Gaudí wasn't without humor, as the most casual glance at Park Güell or the Casa Batlló makes plain. He once burst out laughing when someone compared one of his houses to Hansel and Gretel's.

Echoes of Gaudí's work can be found in the strangest places. Robert Hughes detects it in the sculptures of Claes Oldenburg, and it's probably there in the flaring waves and prows of Frank Gehry's Guggenheim in Bilbao. It certainly predates cubism—which Gaudí also detested—and many another modernism that Antoni would have deplored: not just the "soft machines" of surrealism but vorticism, constructivism, even futurism (those scary militaristic columns in the Sagrada). In pop terms, it can even be seen in the graphic art of H.R. Giger and the "living rock" album sleeve art and architectural projects of Roger Dean.

Yet Antoni Gaudí i Cornet would have disowned them all. Gaudí turned to nature—which he called his greatest teacher—to study what it did to support things—trees, rocks, limbs, bodies both animal and human. He then applied nature's techniques to the buildings he had been asked to build. The results were buildings such as the Casas Batlló and Milà, the crypt of the Colonia Güell, and El Templo Expiatorio de la Sagrada Familia. That these shapes should later turn up in other art movements, and on Yes album sleeves and the set for *Alien*, is coincidence. It suggests, however, that Gaudí saw something deeper and more profound in nature and had the skills to turn it into architecture. Certainly, few other architects have produced work that lives up to Constantin Brancusi's definition of architecture as "inhabited sculpture." It may seem pretentious, and is certainly unusual for an atheist observer to find himself suggesting, but it is almost as though Gaudí's work was a conversation with his God, utterly private and yet conducted in public. That, perhaps, is what made his buildings fly.

PARC DE LA CIUTADELLA *1878–82*

Courtesy of Oronoz

APART from the feeder tank for the park fountain, Gaudí's contribution to the park has never been confirmed. Indeed, given the post of an assistant in the offices of an established architect such as Josep Fontseré i Mestres, we might reasonably expect that his was a fairly lowly role in the making of the park. It was, however, the project that snatched Gaudí from early obscurity, although it is likely that his talents would have made themselves known eventually. There are two reasons for this. The first is that the Parc was the showcase public space for the much-vaunted Eixample, the extension of the old city northwards, designed by radical city planner Ildefons Cerdá. This was a major project in the history of Barcelona, one that would bring space, light, and order to the most overcrowded city in Europe. It was a stroke of luck that Gaudí found himself working on it. The second reason that his contribution would have been recognized eventually is his hidden in the park's fountain.

"Fountain" is something of a misnomer. If anything, it resembles a high mountain torrent in full flood mysteriously transported into the heart of the city. Ten levels of waterfall carry water down to two concentric pools, the whole encircled by extravagant monumental sculpture. It is possible that Gaudí had a hand in the artfully fake rustic stone work in the watercourse. His chief contribution, however, was his calculation that the tank feeding the fountain might collapse. This structural intuition would inform the whole of his work.

As artful and ornate as Gaudí's work was, there is an underlying strength to his creations. He was not just a fanciful draughtsman, he knew what could and couldn't be done with a project in order to make it function properly as well as provide a truly decorative sight. This fountain is as arresting and impressive as any water feature adorning the majestic Renaissance squares of Italy.

LAMPPOSTS, PLAÇA REIAL AND BARCELONETA *1878–89*

Courtesy of Oronoz

THE design for the lampposts that still stand in Barcelona's Plaça Reial, just off the southern end of the Ramblas, suggests that Gaudí was responsible for certain metalwork features in the Parc de la Ciutadella, notably the gates and lights attached to them. The designs are quite similar and, if they are indeed both Gaudí's, already show a confidence and invention with complex metalwork. It would be too early to expect a definitive style to emerge, although already a sense of Gaudí's attitude to history—or what one critic has called "ahistoricity," taking ideas out of their historical context and mixing them with others—could be seen in the park lights, which fused medieval imagery (the knight's helmet, for example) with the contemporary patterning in the gates.

The Plaça Reial lampposts were Gaudí's winning entry for a competition in 1878. Far more elaborate than the Ciutadella lampposts, these also fused traditional forms with contemporary. Most notable, and most visible at the top of each six-sectioned lamppost, is the winged helmet of Mercury, messenger of the gods. In fact, the helmet is part of a larger design theme in the posts—the caduceus, or two serpents twined around a staff topped by the helmet. Today more commonly known as the symbol of the medical profession, the caduceus has a wealth of other symbolisms. The snake—which can signify safety, continuity, eternity, and a number of equally profound negative concepts—proved to be one of the key symbols that Gaudí would employ until the very end of his career.

Although not the first architect to decorate street furniture, Gaudí is surely the most eclectic and impressive. Street lights across Europe have carried fanciful designs on their stems for almost as long as they have existed (witness the fake foliage and ornate green patterning on lampposts in London's Regent's Park and Primrose Hill, for example). Perhaps uniquely, however, Gaudí's lampposts are also designed to cast a strong and far-reaching light along the pavement.

MATARÓ 1881

Courtesy of Prof. Juan Bassegoda Nonell, Real Catedra Gaudí, Barcelona

THE projected communal development for the textile workers' cooperative society La Obrera Mataronense, in the town of Mataró south of Barcelona, was Gaudí's first commissioned building. Some observers have read into the Mataró project evidence of Gaudí's interest in the fledgling socialist movement. Given his subsequent career, this flies in the face of all evidence and most certainly reason.

The cooperative was just one of a variety that sprang up to cope with the drastic shifts in population that occurred during the agricultural decline and industrial boom around Barcelona in the late nineteenth century. Not only was Barcelona the most overcrowded city in Europe, but social conditions surpassed anything described by Dickens or Zola. The Spanish Church supplied some housing and support, although this has been described by some as mere stabling for rapacious industrialists. Some employers, such as Gaudí's future friend and patron, Eusebi Güell i Bacigalupi, even constructed philanthropic workers' settlements on the lines of Britain's Port Sunlight.

Before the Mataró commune fell apart, Gaudí managed to design and oversee the construction of a warehouse. It featured a number of slogans, such as "Nothing is more powerful than brotherhood" and "Comrade! Show solidarity." After the collapse of the cooperative, a disillusioned Gaudí declared himself apolitical, although all his later friendships would be with figures on the religious and industrial right.

The Mataró warehouse does provide us with a keystone, as it were, of his career: the parabolic arch, which soars through all his work. It might also offer a summation of Gaudí's work, from the Hindustani proverb: An arch never sleeps.

CASA VICENS, CARRER DE LES CAROLINES *1883–5*

Courtesy of Oronoz

THE Casa Vicens was Gaudí's first design for a private house, and contains a number of other firsts as well. Despite an obvious debt to Mudéjar and Arabic styles, it sees its creator already moving towards the mature style that would mark later buildings. Situated in what today is a somewhat down-at-heel area of Barcelona, north of the Passeig de Gracia and the Diagonal, the Casa Vicens still manages to stand out in a hodgepodge of urban vernacular and ugly shop fronts.

In 1878, aged 26, Gaudí was commissioned by the wealthy brick manufacturer Manuel Vicens i Montaner to build a townhouse. The floorplan is fairly conventional, although the house "front" actually faces sideways to make the most of the plot, providing garden space (including a fountain removed long ago) and privacy in the main rooms. Several themes that would recur throughout Gaudí's work are immediately established: the purely decorative minaret-like towers of the roof; the rich patterning of tiles; the margallo palm-leaf (or palmetto) motif in the metalwork fencing; the use of parabolic arches in the interior; and corbeled supports on the exterior. Here, Gaudí had his first brush with over-cautious workmen worried that his designs might collapse. A workman warned him that, when complete, the weight of the house would crush the corbels, the cantilever-like brick projections that support the upper galleries of the building. Gaudí assured the workman that he had done his calculations, but the man stayed behind for hours, certain the structure would be damaged. The Casa Vicens stands, intact, 120 years later.

CASA VICENS

EXTERIOR

Courtesy of Oronoz

THE vertical and horizontal lines of the Casa Vicens tilework, the chamfered squares of the rough-dressed stonework, the trefoil—that is, "three-leaved pattern"— balconies, and the free form metalwork give us a good measure of the spatial imagination at work in Gaudí's first house. As well as borrowing from Arabic and Mudéjar styles, Gaudí is juggling with forms here, overlaying, intermixing, and fusing several styles into his own distinctive one.

Already, in this first building, Gaudí's style is assured and confident in its aims, perhaps, it can be argued, it is even arrogant in its assertion.

The *rejillas*, or grilles, on the windows are a common feature of 19th- and even 20th-century Spanish domestic architecture. Their provenance is medieval, and their modern function largely decorative, although their defensive origin is the reason that people in Spain still have bars across their windows.

Spain is neither more nor less troubled by lawlessness than any other European country. Yet no other European culture has made these grilles, somewhat ominous to outsiders, such a part of domestic architecture. Here, Gaudí added an extra medieval touch, with art nouveau flourishes brandishing aggressive spikes, something that would recur in many a later Gaudí building.

There is also an element of fantasy in this design. It is as if an eight-year old child was asked to draw a castle for an imprisoned princess. The playful, innocent colors of the tiles and walls offset the almost terrible threat of pain and imprisonment inherent in the spikes and bars. The checkered tiling brings to mind the chessboard of Lewis Carroll's *Alice in Wonderland*.

CASA VICENS

INTERIOR

Courtesy of Oronoz

ALTHOUGH of a modest size and plan, the Vicens house fizzes with invention. As well as placing his stamp on the city of Barcelona, or at least this *barrio* of it, this was also the first project in which Gaudí designed the interior throughout. The interior is among the most sumptuous in his entire career, due largely, one imagines, to the indulgence of Manuel Vicens i Montaner.

As he would do elsewhere, Gaudí took his complex tiling patterns indoors, both the checker work and the floral themes, and the contrast between the lustrous sheen of glaze and the matte of stonework. Here, however, it was not the crude stonework of the exterior—a Gaudíism that would later take on pronounced cultural and even political symbolism—but the sumptuous Moorish patterning that we can see above this curiously proportioned door and in the columns above the dado rail to either side. These recall the mathematically patterned ceilings of such sites as the Alcázar in Seville or the Alhambra in Granada.

The door itself also hints at another Gaudí innovation. He was already experimenting with his own technique for producing a stained-glass effect, using different layers and thicknesses of colored glass to produce the subtle gradations of color that would themselves become a major part of his work. Although he would work with shades of white—again, largely for symbolic reasons—for Gaudí, color was an inseparable part of architecture.

It is impossible to ignore the suggestion of religiosity in the colored glass employed here. All around Gaudí the churches of Spain contained fantastic stained glass tableaux of magnificent and sometimes brutal scenes (from virgin birth to crucifixion). They are powerful and carry such a strong glow of reverence that the temptation to use the light forms for secular use must have been immense to the young architect. There are no direct links to the church in the colored glass, but still there is a hint.

CASA VICENS

CEILING

Courtesy of Oronoz

TRUE to his belief that every aspect of a house, from the grand plan down to the tiniest detail of decoration and even such "invisible" features as plumbing and sewerage, was all part of an organic whole, Gaudí lavished great detail on the interior of the Casa Vicens. He also essayed an effect that would become another key theme in his work, a witty, almost punning device of quotation, from nature or from other styles, verging on and sometimes entering the world of *trompe l'oeil*. This may seem at odds with his deserved reputation as a naturalist architect, one avowedly committed to the integrity of form and substance, but these conceits or droll asides can be linked to his philosophy of architecture and the emphasis he placed on decoration.

The Moorish and Mudéjar details he fashioned for the interior of the Casa Vicens might almost be considered throwaway when compared to other effects he created in the interior. He garlanded columns with molded fruit, echoed in painted panels for the walls, and hung birds from a ceiling where employing a delicate sense of perspective he transformed a flat surface into what appeared to be a clear glass cupola above which birds appeared to be flying into the sky. These effects would recur throughout his career, reaching a pinnacle, almost literally, in the Sagrada Familia.

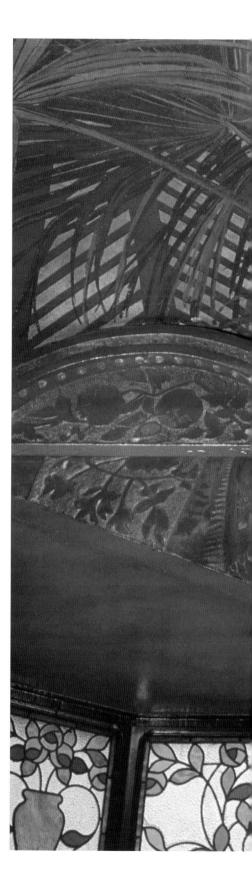

CASA VICENS

EXTERIOR FEATURES

Courtesy of Oronoz

ALTHOUGH it is his first private house, the Casa Vicens sees Gaudí the architect already getting well into his stride. The decision to place the house side-on to the street, in a position entirely at odds with the configuration of any of the other buildings in the Carrer de les Carolines, shows a bold and imaginative use of a restricted space, something he would excel at when shoe-horning the Palau Güell into a tiny plot off the Ramblas. While quoting from other styles, the architect's personal touch is striking and assertive, not least in the tiny *hommage* to his metalworking forebears in the concealed metalwork spiderweb, an allusion to another genius in working in three-dimensional space.

Most striking, however, is that the Casa Vicens façade is covered in writhing snakes—wrought, that is, in iron. The snake is probably the first and most abiding symbol in all Gaudí's work. Beyond its obvious biblical symbolism, it represents health, longevity, creation, nature, eternity, and many more variable readings besides. In Gaudí's work, it would reach its apogee in the snake bench of the Park Güell— where the metalwork palmetto palm leaf would also be precisely and deliberately repeated—and would even feature in the devotional sculpture on the exterior of the Sagrada Familia.

As with the windows of the Casa Vicens, the façade reflects an almost fairytale style. The terror of the quiet, deadly snake contrasts with the wonderful shell-like patterns on the gates. Both symbols of wonder and attraction to the enquiring mind of small children who know fear but not why they fear. There is little risk, one imagines, that the local children would dare to play tricks on the owner of such a strange and fantastical home. Equally, of course, the children of the owner have a marvellous surrounding in which to play games and pretend.

CASA VICENS

TILING

Courtesy of Oronoz

AS well as enhancing the patterned effect of the façade, brickwork was an incredibly cheap way to build a house—especially when the bricks were provided by the owner himself. While some of the checkered tiling owes something to Arabic style, Gaudí allowed himself a personal touch in these exuberantly flowered tiles.

When he first visited the site, it was covered with tiny yellow flowers. Believing that a building should reflect something of its site (the Park Güell would be built in part of rock excavated at the site), he created a design whereby the tiles would climb the walls of the house. There is an almost musical rhythm to the patterning, with the tiles repeating and overlaying each other along diagonal and vertical lines. In fact, the tiling starts in a recognisably Spanish style at the lower level and becomes increasingly Arabic-Mudéjar as it travels up the façade.

Here we also see Gaudí employing what would become other key themes in his work. As well as restoring the yellow flowers to the site, he also used the pattern of a palmetto he found on the site as a recurring motif in the metalwork. It is a motif that would repeat throughout his work. The complex tile patterning is contrasted with deliberately rough stonework, another Gaudí theme.

Gaudí was possibly the first eco-architect in this sense. His use of materials natural to the site on which he built was a conscious effort to marry tradition with the modern. His work is almost post-industrial and radically anti-modern, of course. Yet he would use methods and means which were contemporary to his time and create buildings which were almost impossible to make work with the means available to craftsmen of that period. It was, at times, as if he wanted to see how far he could push the skills of builders for the greater glory of his work. In the same way that the magnificent cathedrals of the middle ages rose far above the uneducated masses from among whom the craftsmen were chosen to work toward the greater glory of that church.

VILLA QUIJANA (EL CAPRICHO) COMILLAS, SANTANDER *1883–5*

Courtesy of Oronoz

EL Capricho—the caprice, or whim—is famously the building that Gaudí did not oversee during its construction. Not only did he not visit the site, he handed the management of the project to a friend. According to his assistant, amanuensis, and biographer Joan Bergós i Massó in his book, *Gaudí, el hombre y la obra*, Gaudí feared that he and its owner, Máximo Diaz de Quijano, might not get on if they met. The reason is bizarre: simply, and perhaps a little superstitiously, because Gaudí thought that Quijano's name was a little too close to "Quijote." Consequently, a fellow student from the School of Architecture, Cristóbal Cascante i Colom, oversaw the project. While contemporary with the Casa Vicens and sharing some of its stylistic themes, El Capricho was an entirely different project: a summer villa for a wealthy bachelor, with a lifestyle requiring a different distribution of space than a businessman's family townhouse. Where the Vicens house had to provide the conventional offices of the home—bedrooms, bathrooms, kitchen, dining room, and so on—El Capricho was a space designed to allow Don Máximo to entertain guests, with the dormitory and service spaces arranged around a large, central salon.

Given a freer rein than at the Vicens site, Gaudí's ideas can already be seen to be flexing their muscles. The tower is no longer the decorative fillip of the Vicens roof but something that could be climbed and looked out of; the ostentatious corbels support a sturdy roof designed solely with the rainy climate of northern Spain in mind; the façade is a riot of detail. Here, Gaudí is stretching the ideas he essayed in the Casa Vicens, becoming bolder in their execution and daring. He is also making his first steps into landscaping in the surrounding terrain: extending the walls of the house into supporting walls in the hillside enclosing outdoor seating areas, "defended" by more ostentatious corbeled brick pillars.

Villa Quijana (El Capricho)

Façade

Courtesy of Oronoz

ALTHOUGH the façade of El Capricho isn't as busy as that of the Casa Vicens, the two houses are stylistically similar, and here, in Gaudí's second commissioned house, more Gaudíisms are beginning to appear.

El Capricho, as the name might suggest, was intended as a playhouse for a wealthy man, and the design appears to be a *recherché* game, with neo-Gothic forms rendered as though the building was constructed of brightly-colored candy sweets. The wealth of color, deployed in geometrical patterns around the façade, prefigures the riotous coloring of the Casa Batlló, and there is more here that seems to look forward to Gaudí's first house in the Eixample. The color-play moves on to the roof, where the terracotta is strikingly contrasted with the glazed green tiling: distant descendants of these would grow globular and rear up on the Casa Batlló roof in a shape suggesting the back of a stegosaurus. Other familiar figures from the Gaudí menagerie are also visible here: the chimneys are clearly related to the visored sentinels guarding the roof of the Casa Milà, and other chimneys by Gaudí, which have a story all of their own.

Villa Quijana (El Capricho)

Sunflower chimneys

Courtesy of Oronoz

THE sunflower chimneys of El Capricho are something of an oddity. From early on in his career, Gaudí was keen to address himself to the less glamorous aspects of a house or building: how its interior and services functioned, and how to integrate water supplies, waste disposal, heat and air vents, and lighting into the desired end design. The Capricho chimneys are clearly related to the dramatic chimneys he would place on later buildings—sometimes in groups that critics have read as alluding to religious sculpture—but the abundance of sunflowers also lends another, almost pagan, element.

Later allusions to occult matter aside, his chimneys seem unambiguously anthropomorphic, or hinting at human forms. They have been compared to the *espantabrujeras*—literally, "witch-scarers"—fashioned on chimneys in the Spanish Pyrenees and elsewhere, human shapes designed to scare witches from landing on the roof. In fact, his chimneys and air vents for his buildings in the center of Barcelona such as La Pedrera were nicknamed the *espantabrujeras*. Yet these glorious haloes of symbolic sunflowers give El Capricho's gaunt watchdogs the air of participants in some celebratory pantheistic ritual.

What is clear, however, is the marriage of modern, almost industrial straight edges with the ornate, clearly handmade decoration that would have been commonplace a century or more earlier. There is little of the fairytale in these chimneys and while there are religious references, there are also militaristic, or certainly defensive, impressions given. Seen from certain angles they could belong to a fortified castle.

At this distance however, it is impossible to decode just what Gaudí was up to on the roof of El Capricho.

VILLA QUIJANA (EL CAPRICHO)

ENTRANCE

Courtesy of Oronoz

THE proportions of El Capricho may make it seem that the caprice or whim was in fact that of the architect. Here, certain dramatic features—tower and mirador, roof, exterior masonry—are even more exaggerated than they were in the Casa Vicens. As well as the mirador atop the tower, more decorative features were launched into space. The gateway, which opens out on to the only project apart from the Park Güell where Gaudí would try his hand at landscaping, is dominated by the coat of arms of the commissioning client whose name inspired Gaudí to hand the project management to a friend. Below it he abandoned his signature parabolas and catenary arches for the most atypical arch in his career, a neo-Gothic stone arch flanked by supporting walls faced with hypnotic tiling patterns echoing the façade of the house itself. Above it we see an example of Gaudí's ability to imagine structures in three dimensions and translate them into the mathematics that would support his plans for his buildings.

Employing what are in fact simple brickwork and corbels, Gaudí fired the ornamental lintels into space, extending what were already extraneous details into a further ornamental flourish. It supplied Don Máximo Diaz de Quijano with a suitably imposing entrance for his summer estate, although some critics have found this last finesse an unnecessary exercise in style. It is one of the few examples of Gaudí's work where innovation, intelligence, and wit give way to bombast, although this may have been at the request of Don Máximo.

If it was for the client, then he clearly has a gate to suit his sense of style.

VILLA QUIJANA (EL CAPRICHO)

WINDOWS

Courtesy of Oronoz

AS WITH the flowers swarming over the Casa Vicens, Gaudí let his sunflowers run riot over the Villa Quijana. He had himself already commented that the flower "is the image of the center and as such the archetypal image of the soul. In alchemy, it symbolizes the work of the sun."

Beyond the decorative effect, Gaudí intended certain aspects of the building to act as a cheering corrective to the climate in northern Spain, where some regions record twice the annual rainfall of England. The thousands of glazed tile sunflowers marching up and across the façade in vertical and horizontal bands, almost as though in a four-square rhythm, clearly have a symbolic meaning. It is possible that here we are seeing the first appearance of references to alchemy and other forms of occult science that seem to hover on the edge of so many of his works.

The sunflower, *girasol* in Spanish, is an emblematic oil crop in Spain and its name is the rough Spanish equivalent of "heliotropic," the Greek-rooted word for any plant that has the curious ability to turn itself towards the sun. Access to sunshine and light—however paradoxical it might be in this cloudiest region of Spain—is a key theme in the decorative program of El Capricho. Even the windows have been stretched out of proportion to suck light into the interior.

As with the chimneys there is a militaristic edge to these sharp-topped windows. Their quartered frames could double as slots through which to point weapons at the advancing enemy. The arrow-shaped tops are hard and edged with tiling to resemble teeth or at least a serrated edge. As much as the sunflowers warm the building it is hard to feel that there is a warm welcome within. The edges and sparseness of color add to the militaristic feel of El Capricho.

Güell Pavilions, Pedralbes *1884–7*

Courtesy of AISA

THE pavilions that Gaudí designed for the Güell family estate mark the emergence of a number of other key themes in his works, and ones that would endure throughout his career. They also bring into play a factor we may overlook when considering Gaudí's work today: situation. While some of his greatest houses, not to mention the Sagrada Familia, were constructed in the heart of the city of Barcelona, many were built in what was still open countryside outside the city. (Another, urban, factor will come into play later: skyline.) We should bear this in mind when considering these works, as their context has been utterly transformed by the expansion of the city.

While today they sit on a busy suburban intersection facing across to modern apartment blocks, the Pavilions Güell were built as the gatehouse, riding hall, and stables of the Güell country estate in Pedralbes. Although commissioned by Eusebi, and roughly contemporary to the construction of his townhouse, the Palau Güell, off the Ramblas, they were built for his father, Joan Güell Ferrer, at the edge of his Can Feliu estate. (It is next to the Parc del Palau Reial de Pedralbes, which has a tiny Gaudí dragon fountain hidden in a bamboo thicket near the monumental fountain in front of the house.)

GÜELL PAVILIONS, PEDRALBES

DRAGON GATE

Courtesy of Oronoz

THE fierce creature defending the gate of the Güell Pavilions crops up as a reference in other areas, most notably in the film *Alien*. While there is no stylistic similarity between this stage of Gaudí's architecture and the designs of the Swiss artist H.R. Giger, Gaudí's later organic and bone-shaped works are an obvious influence on the baleful organic structures of Giger's set and special effects designs for *Alien*, and other artworks of Giger's besides.

The dragon has its own curious mythical provenance, but it is first and foremost a marvel of art nouveau-inspired design and engineering. The gate is a single piece of metalwork, 15 feet high, and its height and weight meant that Gaudí had to anchor it to a gatepost over 30 feet high to stabilize the structure. Those sweeping lines would later turn into the chopper-bike/low-rider curves of the cockpit commanded by the xenomorph in Ridley Scott's film. (It also has a less ferocious cousin guarding the Bodegas Güell at Garraf south of Barcelona.) The gate leads into the gardens of the Güell property, and the dragon hints at a trail of symbols around the façade. Gaudí also built a little trick into the gate, something he would do with other properties. When the gate is opened—which it rarely is; there is an altogether humbler garden gate to the left of the monster's gaping jaws—a chain attached to the limb below its head lifts the claw as though it is about to attack the visitor.

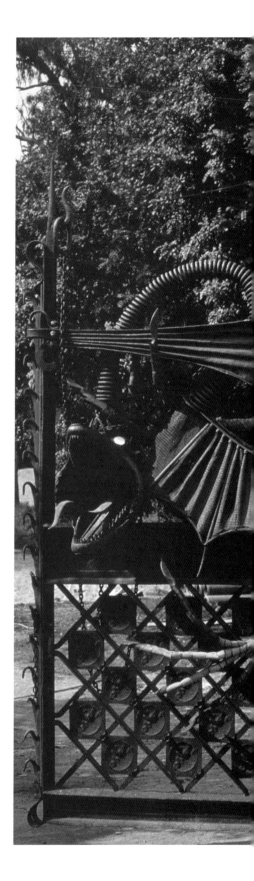

GÜELL PAVILIONS, PEDRALBES

FAÇADE

Courtesy of AISA

ALTHOUGH the façades of the Pavilions share similarities with both the Vicens and El Capricho buildings—highly stylized readings of Arabic design and others from further east—they lack the complexity of either. This mixture would also reach its apogee in the Park Güell. Chiefly, though, the Pavilions are notable as the first Gaudí project to contain explicit symbolic content.

As Robert Hughes points out in his history of the city, *Barcelona*, the dragon may be read as the scaly foe of St George, who had translated to Spanish religious iconography as Sant Jordi with little discomfort. Yet Hughes presents convincing evidence that the dragon—guarding not only a garden but a fruit tree, on the pinnacle above it—is the dragon that protected the Garden of the Hesperides and the golden apples of the sun (although here the apples become Spanish oranges).

The dragon and the apples, subjects of the eleventh Labor of Hercules, feature as a key event in the epic Catalan myth-poem *L'Atlantida* by Jacint Verdaguer, a friend of Gaudí's. *L'Atlantida* is awash with potent symbolism hymning the religious, historic, and mythical origins of Catalanism—not to mention metaphors referring to contemporary Catalan culture and politics.

The Pavilions might almost be seen as an occult guide to the Catalanist movement. (It also worth noting that the myth of Atlantis was popular, as both image and metaphor, among many Catalan poets of this period.) Thus do rubbish, God, and monsters rub shoulders on one humble suburban street corner in modern-day Barcelona. Which is why people still stop, amazed, and literally gawp at this bizarre and fascinating building.

GÜELL PAVILIONS, PEDRALBES

PAVILION ENTRANCE

Courtesy of AISA

PUT crudely, three fundamental Gaudí themes appear in the pavilions: rubbish, God, and monsters. Gaudí built the pavilions on a base of rubble, not only because it was extremely cheap but also because it provided excellent insulation.

It is here that we see the first appearance of a design technique that Gaudí would employ throughout his career: camouflaging simple materials in the skin of something finer, as he would do with clad brick. As well as the "cosmetic" effect, which Gaudí actually believed was integral to his architecture, there was also the added sense of a private conceit in passing off a simple material as something grander. This was one of the themes that would recur in his work.

The Pavilions also give the first hint of Gaudí's alchemical transformation, where a base material is turned into something precious. Rubble, of various sorts, would appear in his later buildings, reaching its apotheosis in the Park Güell. God has a walk-on part in the symbolism at play around the buildings, as he would in many other Gaudí buildings, and we should pause to note the wealth of symbolism in general on display here. Indeed the idea of empires themselves is conveyed by the creation of such grand and ultimately useless pavillions as this (something of which the British too were very fond). What other use has a pavilion except to boast of accomplishment? They are a blatant symbol of imperialism, something of which Gaudí would have disapproved, one thinks.

As we will see later, this is only the opening chapter in what could be seen as an entire book of religious texts that Gaudí wrote, sometimes almost carelessly, into his buildings.

GÜELL PAVILIONS, PEDRALBES

PAVILION ROOFTOPS

Courtesy of Oronoz

ALTHOUGH Gaudí had already begun to experiment with exploding the minaret and with incorporating vegetable forms in El Capricho, other innovations appear in the Güell Pavilions. The roofs of both lodges—designed to incorporate light and air vents into the ceilings of the stables and riding hall—are clearly the forebears of the lodges at the Park Güell, and their deliberate asymmetry hints at the morphing shapes of later Gaudí roofs. These almost humanoid hints of heads and helmets would become explicit in later building projects, where both form and color would take on complex symbolic meaning. The patterning also prefigures the disintegration of form that would become so much a part of his later work.

The echoes of Mudéjar patterning in the walls and tiling conceal subtle changes, not least the wealth of detail applied to the exterior—for example, there are minuscule tile patterns running through the interstices of the brickwork. The crowns of both minaret forms, however, are beginning to move beyond the conventional form, both in structure and design. Tiled, bricked protuberances are taking on a horned appearance, and the tiled cladding is moving away from the rhythmic patterns of Moorish design so pleasing to the eye, and towards abstraction and even the dismantled patterns of the later *trencadis* (from the Catalan verb "trencar," to break) mosaic designs. The air vent furthest to the left, the most obvious example of this development, also appears to have been crowned with a clump of what from a distance resemble prickly pear.

GÜELL PAVILIONS, PEDRALBES

INTERIOR

Courtesy of Oronoz

WHILE the exteriors rehearse themes from earlier work—sumptuous rhythmic geometric patterns, pulsing flower motifs and almost ridiculous medieval crenellations—the two most interesting features of the Pavilion interiors, and also to be recurrent in Gaudí's work, are light—and water. Or perhaps wind and sand …

Gaudí was a separatist even when it came to the sunlight, although he generously credited it to the rest of the Mediterranean littoral as well. He disparaged northern European art as soulless and clinical, and once famously said: "The sun is the great painter of the Mediterranean lands." Like Caravaggio, he favored mid-afternoon light, particularly at 45 degrees: "The light that best defines solids and reveals their form."

Consequently, he built both stables and riding hall to maximize light while also defending the space against glare. Windows, grids, and opened cupolas bathe both with a light that remains even through much of the day. In the riding halls, he turned his attentions to the ceiling. Here, Gaudí triggered a *terremoto*, earthquake, across the surface of the ceiling, something he would do with other ceilings, most notably the Casa Milà. He laid a series of half pipes for the roof of the stables, smoothing the undersides to resemble waves, or material ruffled by wind. In the Milà and elsewhere, these would come to resemble dunes suspended upside down in space, or the whorls of whipped cream.

PALAU GÜELL, CALLE NOU DE LA RAMBLA *1886–9*

Courtesy of AISA

GAUDÍ'S townhouse for Eusebi Güell coincided with one of the greatest celebrations of Barcelona and, by extension, Catalan culture, the Universal Exposition held in Barcelona in 1898. Gaudí's amanuensis Joan Bergós describes it as the "stately culmination" of his Moorish–Mudéjar period, and he certainly ended it with a flourish. As befitted a recently ennobled aristocrat—Güell was by now the Conde Güell, thanks to his friendship with the king, Alfonso XII, himself a keen proponent of the Catalan renaissance—this was to be an opulent townhouse reflecting Güell's status and wealth. That is, as much as Gaudí could get into a site measuring merely 54 feet by 66.

The situation of the house was itself curious. Carrer Nou de la Rambla is situated in the area off the Ramblas that was, until a decade or so ago, Barcelona's red-light district and at the time of its construction a dubious part of the city, even so close to the Ramblas. The choice of this plot was probably influenced by its proximity to another Güell property right on the Ramblas. The Palau was actually linked to this other property by a tunnel, suggesting a certain security mindedness in the design which is evident from aspects of the building. (One apocryphal story has it that Gaudí suggested a moat around the entrance but realized this would be impossible, not least because of the high water table in this area.)

If the Palau Güell marks the culmination of his Moorish–Mudéjar phase, it also sees a number of key Gaudí themes asserting themselves. These include the parabolic arch, which would be a feature throughout his career, explicit Catalanist symbolism, mushroom motifs celebrating don Eusebi's hobby of mycology, or mushroom collecting, and Gaudí's bizarre fruit/tree forms, which would reach their apogee in the upper spaces of the Sagrada Familia.

PALAU GÜELL, CARRER NOU DE LA RAMBLA

ENTRANCE

Courtesy of AISA

THE façade of the Palau Güell is more restrained that any of Gaudí's previous private houses, although the interior would more than compensate in its often mind-boggling extravagance. Apart from the sensual, almost organic shapes of the twin parabolic arches, the most striking detail is the wealth of metalwork and, at its center, possibly the first, and certainly the most striking, appearance of the Catalan flag in Gaudí's architectural work. The flag had an almost delirious symbolism for the Catalanist movement.

Robert Hughes explains that this simple but powerful flag—four diagonal red lines on a field of yellow—was originally the coat of arms of the ninth-century warrior count Guifré el Pélos, aka Wilfred the Hairy. Wilfred was the figure who made Barcelona the capital of a unified Catalonia in the medieval era that so enchanted the Catalanists.

The design originates from an incident during a siege against Barcelona in which Wilfred was bloodily wounded. King Louis the Pious, for whom Wilfred was fighting, noticed that Wilfred's shield was simple and unadorned, covered in gold leaf. Intending to praise Wilfred's bravery, Louis dipped his fingers in Wilfred's blood and drew them across the shield, thus creating the bars and an emblem of Wilfred's heroism. Hughes goes on to explain that the two men weren't even contemporaries, and that the anecdote is entirely fictional. That, however, didn't deter generations of Catalanist orators and poets from invoking the blood of Guifré el Pelós as part of the creation-myth of Catalonia. Here, visitors aren't merely admiring a piece of fancy metalwork: this is the Catalanist equivalent of the Holy Grail.

PALAU GÜELL, CARRER NOU DE LA RAMBLA

REAR VIEW

Courtesy of AISA

BOTH the rear and front façades of the Palau Güell were designed with privacy as well as security in mind. The sheer number of columns in the interior was, it would seem, intended to lend a church-like atmosphere to the building, in particular its central hall with its dizzying cupola. The rows of columns in front of the windows overlooking the street also acted as a kind of blind, to further deter prying eyes. (There was a further, faintly spooky, security device built into the house: the Visitors' Room, a reception area for guests off the main hall, had, in the manner of a harem or Arabic palace, a secret upper gallery running around it from which the inhabitants could spy on visitors.) The back elevation, with its robust metal screenings, was actually a defensive installation to deter intruders.

There is also something unusual in the rear elevation of the Palau Güell. A row of air vents along the lowest level of the screening, at the height of the rear terrace and designed to ventilate the stables below, displays distinctly bone- or branch-like forms, their art nouveau-esque apertures suggestive of mouths or internal organs. This too seems to look forward to the anthropomorphic shapes of the Casas Batlló and La Pedrera.

It is clearly another reference to the bloody history of the Catalans and a time when intrigue, whispers, and rumor were weapons as powerful as the sword. The vents are almost a reminder of how many people died for the Catalan cause, the flesh and bones of the dead are the metaphorical infrastructure of the building. It is as if Gaudí is making another anti-imperialist statement. Pavilions were built on rubbish, but the foundations of the homes of the great Catalans are made of human suffering and ultimate sacrifice.

Palau Güell, Carrer Nou de la Rambla

Interior cupola

Courtesy of AISA

THERE'S a famous story about Eusebi Güell's personal secretary complaining to his employer that, in the work on the Palau, señor Gaudí seemed to be spending Güell's money as fast as Güell was making it. Glancing over the receipts proffered by his secretary, Güell is alleged to have snorted: "Is that all he's spending?"

No expense was spared on the Conde's new palace, which would become so famous that even the American press would comment on it. In a unique move that hinted at either a very close relationship with his client, or the opposite, Gaudí broke his own rule about favoring cheap materials native to the site and used polished Garraf marble throughout. It is a material that heightens the religious atmosphere of the building. Today, however, the effect is almost oppressive: living here would be like living in an incredibly ornate corner of a museum.

For the crowning point, quite literally, of his greatest Moorish–Mudéjar design, Gaudí decided, after much alteration of the design, on a classic Moorish touch, the Moorish dome pierced with apertures to introduce light. This central hall, located next to the music room, includes a curious small chapel that opens out into the hall for communal prayer. It could be argued that the quasi-religious duomo effect sought to parody the hypocritical piety of Gaudí's client, with the architect insinuating that the man thought he was, if not actually God, clearly as rich as Him.

The hall was originally planned as a single-storey room. After Gaudí's revisions, as if to outspend his client's earning capacity, it rose two further storeys, and in fact reaches beyond the level of the roof, where the cupola starts to allow light to enter this miniature domestic cathedral.

The reaction of Güell's personal secretary to the finished article is unfortunately not recorded for posterity. There's little doubt, however, that the cupola provides a fantastic space in which to worship the power of what money can buy.

PALAU GÜELL, CARRER NOU DE LA RAMBLA

SALON

Courtesy of AISA

THE space below the cupola was the center of family life in the Palau. The "nave" gave on to a musicians' gallery and was used to accommodate a small orchestra or ensemble during entertainments that Güell liked to stage. In a more private mode, two vast doors opposite the gallery actually opened on to what amounts to a fold-out chapel—something smaller than an ante-room but much larger than a cupboard, dressed in the manner of an elaborate altar. A harmonium-like organ to the side would provide the accompaniment. To the rear of the space, doors open on to a long dining room with a large, almost baronial, fireplace which features Gaudían monsters appearing out of the carved woodwork.

Although both Gaudí and Güell died before the event, the Palau was to have one of the sorriest histories of all of Gaudí's buildings. Positioned so close to the Ramblas, it was a natural target for attack when the numerous factions in the Civil War engaged the military in house-to-house battles along and around the Ramblas (by which time the family had long ago decamped to safer lodgings). The Palau was seized by an anarchist group who used it as their base during the fighting, and among the structural damage wreaked on this symbol of Barcelona's wealthy elite was the destruction of a large statue on the altar. Although the building has now been restored, the statue was never uncovered and has not been replaced.

Of course, the lack of personal information about the architect means that it is virtually impossible to tell how Gaudí would have reacted to such treatment of his buildings. It is possible that he would have enjoyed the the idea of anarchists using the faux cathedral as a center of operations for an assault on the forces of law and order. It's just as possible, of course, that the anarchist view of God would have distressed him immensely.

PALAU GÜELL,
CARRER NOU DE LA RAMBLA

CELLAR

Courtesy of AISA

WHILE Gaudí was designing el Conde Güell's pleasure dome upstairs, he was also planning some monumental work underground. Although the moat was abandoned, the entrance allowed space for horses and carriages to pass into a small courtyard. Guests would mount the stairs to the upper salons; drivers, horses, and carriages would take a steep spiral cobbled ramp down into the cellar, which was a stables with dormitory spaces for servants, who had their own separate cobbled spiral down into this space. (To his credit, Gaudí paid particular attention to ventilation and sluiceways in this area.) This feature, of allowing vehicles into the house, for inhabitants and visitors to ascend to the living space while vehicles and their drivers descended into the cellar, would be repeated, in a far more stylized fashion, in the Casa Milà.

To support the structure above, he fashioned fat mushroom columns, a somewhat recondite pun on the Conde's hobby of mycology (not least because inhabitants and guests would never see the below-stairs area). These monolithic feet of the building, hinting also at tree shapes and the even more extreme supports he would launch into space at Güell's Colonia south of Barcelona, were linked by that other signature shape of Gaudí's work, the catenary arch. The effect is of a forest, either of giant mushrooms or stone trees, something that in fact bursts into flower on the roof.

Palau Güell,
Carrer Nou de la Rambla

Hall

Courtesy of Oronoz

THE stately culmination of Gaudí's Moorish–
Mudéjar period reached its apex, fittingly enough, in
the ceiling of the Palau Güell hall. Key Gaudí themes
recur here in perhaps their most sensuous form. The
parabolic arches framing the windows overlooking
the Carrer Nou de la Rambla are here purely
decorative, although with a secondary purpose: to
screen the lives inside from the prying eyes of
outsiders. They serve no structural function
whatsoever. The corbel ceiling features and elaborate
Moorish detailing in the ceiling themselves seem
intended to conjure up the grandeur of a caliph's
palace—a fitting decorative tribute to the recently
ennobled Conde Güell. To the right, also supported
by elaborately decorated corbels, we see one of the
most curious details in an architectural career replete
in curious detail: the inverted cloister, suspended
from the ceiling, and screened in Moorish-pattern
woodwork.

The diagonally-patterned screens meant that
members of the household could eavesdrop or even
spy on visitors. This was in all probability a stylistic
fancy on the part of Gaudí, but it seems to feed into
the theory that there is a security system of sorts
running through the entire building.

PALACIO GÜELL, CARRER NOU DE LA RAMBLA

CHIMNEYS

Courtesy of AISA

THE modern-day viewer might suspect that the roof of the Palau Güell is the result of Picasso and Miró having one hell of a party up there while Güell was away somewhere. Vegetable shapes had already begun to appear on Gaudí's roofs, and the tiling had begun to fragment towards the abstract *trencadis* of the Park Güell. Yet nothing in his previous work gave a warning of what would clad the chimneys and ventilation hoods on the roof of the Palau.

Not all of the pinnacles—the blue and white cluster of what might be dodecahedrons, for example—are from Gaudí's designs. Yet some, notably the central green tree or honeycomb, recur across the heights of the Sagrada Familia. Curiously, also, the chimneys and air vents of the Palau roof no longer resemble the *espantabrujeras* that first appeared on the roof of El Capricho. In fact, they look like mutant table lamps. (Admirers of Miró will recognize similarities in the dots and wavy lines of the pinnacle to the left of the tree.) Again, however, it would be wrong to read a departure into abstraction in Gaudí's intentions for the Palau roof.

It is entirely possible that this roofscape, which wouldn't look amiss in a de Chirico painting, is in fact a stylized tribute to the hugely popular Jocs Florals movement of the Catalan renaissance. The Jocs Florals—Floral Games—was a poetry festival and street carnival intended to celebrate Catalan tradition. Part of the celebrations involved parades in which participants carried brightly decorated banners atop tall poles. Gaudí designed one such banner for the Jocs Florals, and Güell was also involved in the organisation of the event.

What better way, then, to complete the Conde's Palau than by staging a permanent Jocs Florals carnival on its roof?

PALACIO DE ASTORGA *1887–93*

Courtesy of Oronoz

THE Episcopal Palace at Astorga, León, holds the dubious distinction of being the only Gaudí building to have fallen down, and that because someone else tampered with his designs. It also set a precedent for what one critic has said became a "trademark" in Gaudí's work: that he failed to complete many of his commissions, often due to disputes, misunderstandings or financial or political problems.

The first thing that the Episcopal Palace should draw our attention to, however, is Gaudí's relationship with the man who commissioned him to design it, Juan Bautista Grau i Vallespinós, bishop of Astorga. Grau, a fellow citizen of Reus, asked Gaudí to design a new "palace" for the bishopric of Astorga after the original was destroyed in a fire. Gaudí developed a close friendship with Grau over the six years it took to develop the project and credited Grau with introducing him to daily religious study, something he would devote himself to until the end of his life. Although his key religious mentor would be Josep Torras i Bagès, described by Robert Hughes as a "formidable right-wing cleric," it was Grau who set Gaudí on the path to beatification.

Unfortunately, the episcopal palace at Astorga was also one of the unhappiest projects in Gaudí's career. Its status as a public and religious monument, a prestigious home for a powerful religious figure, meant that it had to undergo the scrutiny of various committees. Regional and aesthetic factionalism bedeviled the project, although there are suggestions that Gaudí's own high-handedness may also have provoked local antipathy. The building's sorry fate was sealed when Grau died before its completion, leaving it to the less than tender mercies of Church officials. Gaudí and his team were dismissed and another architect completed the work.

PALACIO DE ASTORGA

FAÇADE

Courtesy of Oronoz

THE Palacio Episcopal wholeheartedly embraces north European Gothic while at the same time twisting its arm to make it produce the effects Gaudí was seeking in his architecture. Already, the arched entry porch is quoting back to the helmets of the Capricho chimneys and forward to the sentinels atop La Pedrera. The chief impression, however, is of medieval castellation—spires, turrets, snowy crenellations. This underlines a subtler theme running through Gaudí's work: quotation, perhaps even intertextuality, where a work quotes from an earlier work, the loan of the earlier reference pointing up an irony in the work at hand. This is, to quote the critic Ignasi de Solà-Morales, "neo-medievalism"—not, as Gaudí's architectural mentor Viollet-le-Duc had insisted, merely repeating the past, slavishly copying its ideas, but adapting it to the modern day. There is no doubt, however, that this style, also known as "neo-Gothic" and a marked departure from Gaudí's secular designs, is also intricately linked to Gaudí's perception of Catalan history and its presence in the Catalan culture of his era. It is also worth noting, as Solà-Morales points out, that these "neo" references to earlier styles were often quite fraudulent, bearing little relation to the source being quoted, and often perpetrated for ideological reasons, as would become clear in Gaudí's later works.

Palacio de Astorga

Façade/entrance

Courtesy of Oronoz

GAUDÍ'S "neo-Gothicism" is immediately apparent in the entrance to the Episcopal Palace. Where a simple doorway might have sufficed as the ingress to this private residency for a regional bishop, Gaudí decked it out with the panoply of a structure from Arthurian (or, more accurately, Catalan-Medieval) mythology. As well as quoting the *espantabrujeras* of El Capricho and presenting a gigantic foreshadowing of the helmeted sentinels atop La Pedrera, the portico also quotes Gaudí's own tell-tale parabolic arch. Here it is presented in a complex three-dimensional section, sliced out of a cylindrical groundplan at a curving angle to produce the pointed outer arch. The parabola is recessed into a further, interior, arch. Only then does this artifice actually lead on to a conventional doorway.

The neo-Gothic effect continues above the entrance, not least in the trefoil form at the top of the tall, slender windows (themselves in groups of three, suggesting a certain religious symbolism, perhaps alluding to the Holy Trinity, at play around the façade). There is also more than an allusion to the flying buttress, however muted, in the sloping support columns in the structure.

We might also consider the function of the ceremonial balcony above the entrance, a detail replete with meaning in a building such as this. Its position in the overall plan and theme of the building suggests that it is intended for speech-giving or the reviewing of troops, which would seem a purely literary flourish for the bishop's private residence here inside its own secured grounds. (Given the uncertain climate of the region and the sobriety of his job title, it is unlikely that the bishop was a keen sunbather.)

The angels facing the entrance are also of interest: are they guarding the bishop, or are they merely an audience facing the balcony? On the few occasions where Gaudí used angels, he insisted that they be wingless and thus more human in form. That he should give these two wings suggests more subtle or ironic play on Gothic/religious themes.

PALACIO DE ASTORGA

INTERIOR

Courtesy of Oronoz

GAUDÍ chose white granite to emphasize the austerity of the bishop's palace, and before the project was engulfed in disputes, had intended to carry the white up on to the roof. While it is described by some as his defining "Gothic" building, indeed as possibly the greatest example of the genre in Spain, it also retains echoes of the Mudéjar style that so marked his previous works.

The exterior has been described as aggressively dour, but in the interior waves of geometric patterns, elegant arches and flower motifs flow through the various offices of the bishop's ill-fated palace. (In fact, following the disastrous alterations to Gaudí's original plans, the building wasn't completed for opening until the 1960s.) These rise to a climax in the chapel and the throne room. The former is almost riotously ornate, an orgy of gold and green, scallop windows and religious texts (not the first time Gaudí wrote on one of his buildings—that was Mataró—but the first religious graffiti he left behind him). The latter, while no less restrained, recalls the busy verticals of the Vicens exterior in its ascending panels of stained glass.

The intended austerity of this interior is in such marked contrast with earlier work that one cannot help but feel that Gaudí was making a deliberate statement here. It might have been that he felt it necessary to lend his work some gravitas in order to be taken more seriously than before by the outside world. Or he might simply have been in awe of such an illustrious client and man truly close to God (rather than to God's banker). This could be a genuine attempt on Gaudí's part to recreate the medieval cathedrals which are so impressive and imposing; both attributes he had strived to achieve throughout his career.

COLEGIO DE SANTA TERESA DE JESÚS *1889–94*

Courtesy of Oronoz

WHEN Gaudí was commissioned to build a school and accommodation for the nuns of the Order of Saint Teresa of Ávila it was his first avowedly religious work. Until now, contemporary reports describe him as both apolitical and uninterested in religion, although the circles he and Eusebi Güell were moving in had already introduced him to powerful religious figures such as Bishop Juan Bautista Grau i Vallespinós. The project was constrained by a number of factors—the self-imposed poverty of the Teresian order, the austerity of its philosophy and lifestyle—as well as by more prosaic considerations: the first floor was already in existence, and Gaudí inherited someone else's rather simple rectangular floorplan. He was limited by budget and the Teresians' demands for a modest, unembellished building, but still managed to infiltrate some of his own ideas. It is entirely possible that he accepted the commission as a challenge: asking the designer of El Capricho to build a house for the wives of God is akin to asking I. M. Pei or Richard Rogers to design a scout hut.

Colegio de Santa Teresa de Jesús

Façade

Courtesy of AISA

EVEN in its original, semi-rural setting, a short distance from the Güell Pavilions, the Colegio de Santa Teresa was Gaudí's first building constructed, as it were, off-limits. There is no public access to the enclosed order's college and offices, and today mature trees in the extensive grounds block all but the upper floors from public view. In a brief return to earlier work, there is an element of the fairytale in the strangely thrilling entrance. It echoes a cave with its half-concealed arch and spiky, exotic carved gates of cold metal. It is as if Gaudí is making a point of the dedication of those who dare to cross this threshold; those who enter must believe in their safety in the arms of the Lord.

Despite the budgetary and aesthetic restrictions, Gaudí still managed to introduce two of his most beloved architectural devices—the parabolic arch and the helical column—fully-fledged into the design. The parabolic arch—glimpsed here in the main entrance, in the first-floor windows from outside the building, and in the interior corridors—would recur in his work up until his death.

Although restricted financially and by the ascetic philosophy of the Teresian order, the Colegio is in fact one of the purest of Gaudí's works. If anything, the lack of funds concentrated Gaudí's attention on the need to design a large building using simple red brick, and the Colegio is a monument to the humble brick (and the only Gaudí building built almost entirely in undressed brick).

Perhaps unsurprisingly, the project was also not without teething problems. As well as complaining about Gaudí's excessive designs, the order fell out with the architect over his refusal to incorporate a private chapel into the building. Gaudí objected to the idea of building a place of worship that would exclude the general public. Perhaps that forbidding gate and lack of truly decorative color is a reflection of his displeasure with the order's instructions.

COLEGIO DE SANTA TERESA DE JESÚS

ENTRANCE

Courtesy of Oronoz

THE metalwork gate in the doorway to the Colegio is another Gaudí curio. In architectural terms, it is an extravagance of both design and defense, not least because, this far across a wide lawn from high perimeter walls unscalable except by ladders, the sisters of this order bound by a rule of poverty would not have had much worth stealing. (There is also a perfectly sound weather-proof wooden door between the gate and the interior.) It seems that this was one of the details of style to which the order objected so forcefully. Which can only have made Gaudí more determined to produce what we now see.

Although it can be explained in terms of the architect reigning in the excesses of Gothic style, the gate is also interesting in its literal and figurative proximity to a wilder neighbor, the near-contemporary metalwork monster guarding the gate of the Pavilions Güell less than a mile away in Pedralbes. This design is remarkably subdued compared to the malevolent invention on the Pavilion gate. Yet it seems as though the gate's constituent parts—those ambiguous plant or palm fronds, the hints of claw, the whiplash coils and the explicit barbs—could reconstitute themselves into something far nastier if necessary. The nouveau-esque flourishes are harmless, although those spiked sunbursts seem chiefly defensive in their design and position. The whole is dominated by a tall Romanesque cross, but even that is clad in barbs. This far from those imposing perimeter walls, its unambiguous message—stay out or be very sure of why you are entering—seems to have been intended almost as an assurance for those inside the building. That, or to confirm the seclusion of the Teresian order.

COLEGIO DE SANTA TERESA DE JESÚS

HALLWAY

Courtesy of AISA

IN the manner of a piece of music, the entrance to the Colegio states individual themes that will be repeated later, sometimes, as seems to have been Gaudí's wont, in almost hypnotic repetitions. Chief of these, as we shall see, is the parabolic arch first seen in the entrance.

The entrance hall itself boasts a single, solitary, parabolic arch, framed at the end of a long hallway. Given the intensity with which Gaudí applied this style of arch to the two upper floors, this might almost be seen as a teasing allusion before the main Wagnerian theme proper enters.

As if to compensate for the dark and forbidding entrance to the Colegio, the hallway was designed, like the rest of the building, with light in mind: hence the large window above the arch, and the absence of other arches that would have obscured light. Hence, too, the over-extended ceiling heights: Gaudí took the ceilings to almost double-storey height on every floor and, naturally, in every room, although there is obviously an ecclesiastical symbolism at work here: these spaces are deconsecrated naves.

Most curious, however, are the vestigial lampshades, a mutated form of the simple geometric metalwork shapes common in Spanish lighting fixtures even today. These crooked, asymmetical tangles of metal and chain prefigure the disintegrated natural forms that would appear in the stone and metalwork of some of his greatest buildings. They are reminders that although God gave us light, man has had to imitate His work and in doing so created something unnatural and without the warmth or life-giving properties of God's light. Like his lampposts, these lamps are ornate and beautiful but wholly unnatural.

COLEGIO DE SANTA TERESA DE JESÚS

UPPER CORRIDOR

Courtesy of Oronoz

GAUDÍ intensified his use of parabolic arches on the first floor of the Colegio to a point where the impact is almost hallucinatory—perhaps not the effect desired by the religious authorities who commissioned it. Here the arches were surfaced and painted with whitewash, and interior light wells would subtly alter the shade in each space between the arches. It seems unlikely that Gaudí intended this effect, since science hadn't yet acquired this vision, but the receding parabolic arches on this floor recall the perspectives of human internal organs seen through microphotography.

Curiously, the *New England Journal of Medicine*, in its edition of 13 April 1988, seemed to agree, although it is entirely possible that the item it published may have been intended for its 1 April edition. Two colonic specialists had visited the attic of Gaudí's Casa Milà, which employs arches resembling those in the Colegio, and were stunned by its similarity to a photograph of an endoscopy cross-section of the human colon, which they published alongside a photo of Gaudí's arches. Perhaps the surgeons' photograph inspires the comparison, which certainly hadn't been invited by Gaudí's earlier work, but shortly afterwards his buildings would begin to assume an extraordinarily anthropomorphic form.

SPANISH FRANCISCAN MISSION, TANGIER (UNBUILT) *1892–3*

Courtesy of the Institut Amatller d'Art Hispánic

DESPITE his distinctly unhappy experiences with earlier ecclesiastical buildings, in 1892 Gaudí began drafting plans for a Franciscan Catholic mission in the Moroccan capital, Tangier. As the name suggests, this was intended as a bulwark of Christianity in an overwhelmingly Islamic society, and as can be seen Gaudí not only made concessions to indigenous architecture but actively sought to incorporate it in his plans. The dominant feature, the nine major towers in the frontage surrounded by numerous lesser towers, obviously prefigures the towers of the Sagrada Familia, in particular the contrariwise spirals at left and right and also in the perimeter wall in the background.

Perhaps sensitive to the cultural distance between Barcelona and Tangier, Gaudí refrained from any explicit Christian references on the exterior. Some of his key themes—the neo-Gothic windows on the towers, the monumental two-storey parabolic arch in the entrance, the corner towers—are easily recognized even in this preparatory sketch. The two floors of windows in the façade, however, suggest that Gaudí is reaching back to his early Mudéjar influences. This continues in the long row of narrow windows on the ground floor, echoing the windows of houses such as the Vicens and the Palau Güell and suggesting in their arrangement an interior courtyard or cloister. It was never built—the reason is unknown, although it is likely that this too fell foul of Church planning committees—but it would have been the only Gaudí building outside Spain.

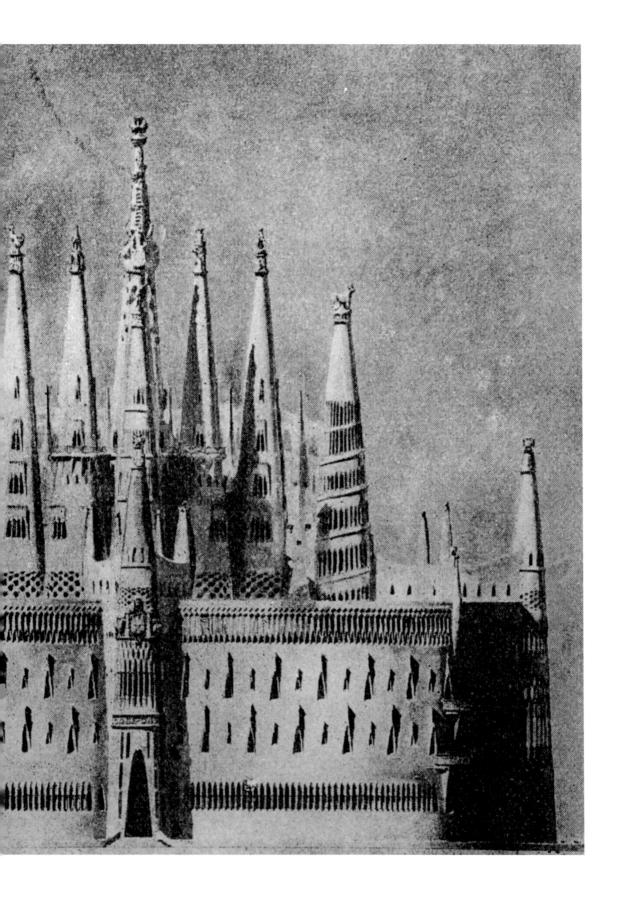

CASA DE LOS BOTINES, LEÓN *1892–4*

Courtesy of Oronoz

WHILE he was working on the Palacio Episcopal in Astorga, Gaudí was also commissioned to build what would perhaps be his most secular building: an office block cum apartment development for the Fernandez-Andres family. They lend their name to the Casa de los Botines' local nickname, the Casa Fernandez. (More confusingly, the Botines came from the surname of the project's financier, Joan Homs i Botinàs.)

Here, Gaudí's neo-Gothicism seems to be approaching a state of delirium, one made all the more notable by the fact that the Casa de los Botines is a dramatic, free-standing structure set in the middle of a town, León, noted for its Renaissance architecture. While its architectural program is severe (if tending towards a certain hysteria as we approach the roof and the spires of the signature corner towers), the bare stonework of the façade appears in certain lights to be made of candy, or biscuit. Some modern viewers will find their thoughts tugged towards the turreted fancies of Walt Disney. (The idea of an office block being a veritable castle against corporate raiding is a very modern one enjoyed by many, particularly fantastical filmmaker Terry Gilliam.)

That, however, was far from the architect's intention, as one or two details convey. Knowing that León experienced heavy snows in winter, Gaudí deliberately exaggerated the angles of the roof and spires; the results brought crowds of onlookers after the first winter snows following its completion.

The interior was designed to be entirely functional: storage spaces in the basement, suites of offices above and apartments in the top floors. The roof also conceals some surprises—twelve, in fact—grouped black chimneys resembling the vents of organ pipes but also chillingly futuristic in their military mien. And then there's the chap over the door.

CASA DE LOS BOTINES, LEÓN

SCULPTURE

Courtesy of Oronoz

LIKE the Casa Vicens and its cherubs perched on the exterior, the Casa de los Botines boasts a sculpture that underlines the collaborative nature of all architecture. As colleagues, collaborators, assistants and workmen would later implement Gaudí's designs, mosaics, and representational sculptures on and around his buildings, so here he worked with the sculptor Matamala to create a distinctive and suitably austere centerpiece for this imposing—if not indeed altogether frightening—façade.

Where the parentage of the roaring terror on the gate of the Güell Pavilions has been traced to the chained dragon guarding the Garden of the Hesperides, this beast—unequivocally a crocodile, or perhaps alligator—is the mythic dragon being slain by Saint George. George—or Jordi, as he became known after he passed passport control—first appeared in Spanish mythology in the sixteenth century, when a fashion for Anglophilia saw other figures from British history and myth also being adopted by the Catalans, who made Jordi/George their patron saint. Jordi would also translate into the potent brew of Catalanist myth-making promoted by figures such as Jacint Verdaguer. Jordi would later show up on the façade of the school built in the shadow of the Sagrada Familia, the better, Gaudí said, to educate Barcelona's children about their patron saint. It's likely that Gaudí's act of exporting the Catalan patron saint to León has a subtler symbolism whose full meaning is lost to us today.

BODEGAS GÜELL *1895–1901*

Courtesy of AISA

THE Bodegas Güell, built near the shore of the seaside town of Garraf south of Barcelona, is one of Gaudí's less well-known projects. Yet it illustrates a number of fascinating themes in both Gaudí's work and professional career, and shows how certain factors influenced each other in his life.

First, the Bodegas Güell is not, as the name might imply, a wine cellar or winery. (Given the lifestyles and philosophies of architect and patron, and the nature of this building, that would have been virtually unthinkable.) The Bodegas was a social center built as a gesture of thanks to the workers in the Garraf quarries, who produced much of the stone Gaudí worked with in his Barcelona projects. There were, and still are, various quarries being worked in Garraf—one of them owned by Eusebi Güell. Gaudí visited the quarries regularly, to check the quality and color of the stone being quarried there.

The Bodegas, or cellar, was designed as one large hall—a magnificent space supported by a large-scale version of Gaudí's signature parabolic arch—with a small balcony and service rooms, intended to be used for meetings and social events. Aptly, today it is a very popular weekend restaurant, although hemmed in by the coast road and train lines, which arrived some time after Gaudí's death. Although these detract from the effect, the medieval watchtower (to which the building is deliberately linked by a raised stone walkway) anchors the modern structure in the past, when this would have been a wild rocky shoreline.

The modern use of the space for eating, drinking, and distinctly secular activity is perhaps a direct contrast to the non-secular image presented by the arches and faux altar shown here. The lack of light echoes the idea of a chapel in which God's light can be seen metaphorically rather than actually. It can also, of course, appear that the space is a perfect underground bar in which men can meet, drink, and converse, away from prying, disapproving eyes, as well as providing good cover from harsh weather and high winds. All of this must have struck those who turned it into a restaurant.

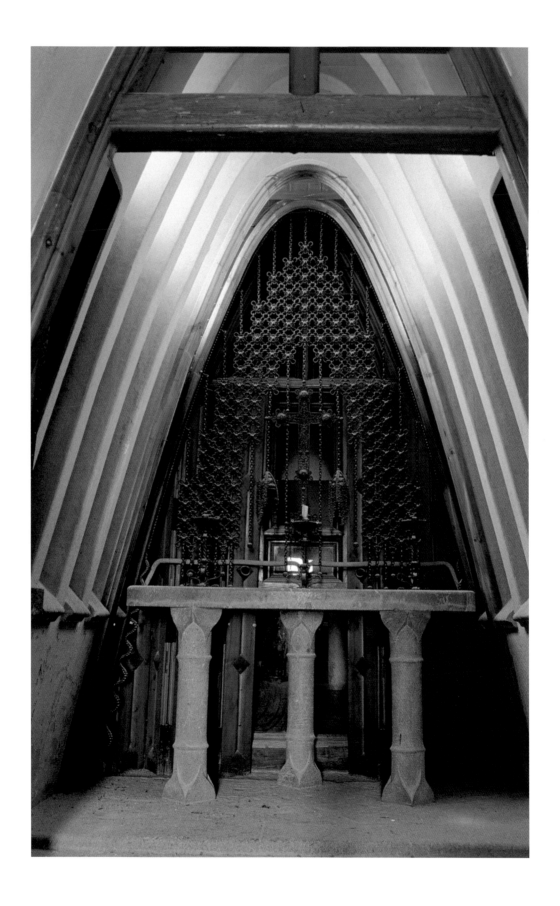

Bodegas Güell

Exterior

Courtesy of AISA

ALTHOUGH this is in fact Gaudí's most southerly building, the simple, almost bivouac shape, the steep neo-Gothic roof, and the use of rough-hewn local granite all hark back to his neo-Gothic palaces in the north of Spain. This is an impressive, large, imposing building which could be both a secular meeting place and a church—albeit one which was hewn from granite by apparently unskilled craftsmen intent on function more than fancy.

Given its intended function as a community meeting place, the exposed seaward balcony is a whimsical detail on a par with his earlier minarets and towers: fewer than half a dozen people could actually fit into the drastic angles of this space. Yet it seems likely that this feature was intended to, if only symbolically, open the space up to the sea and the power of nature.

The Bodegas contains two striking features that are rarely, if ever, seen in published photographs: stone chimneys and air vents along the apex of the roof that display the morphing qualities of his Barcelona rooftop features, and also allude to crosses and other arcane symbols. And the gate to the property is a "soft machine" version of the famed dragon gate: a heavy net of loose iron chain hung from a frame that hints at animal bone structures, in a single gate swinging on a tall gatepost just like that at the Güell Pavilions. This one looks relatively harmless, but it is definitely a relative of the monster guarding the Güell estate at Pedralbes.

There is another, subtler, subtext at work here. Although his patron owned one of the quarries, Gaudí favored Garraf stone for a number of his works. The influence has never been definitively identified, but the cliffs around Garraf and the gouged quarry workfaces have been claimed as one of the influences on the façade of Casa Milà (La Pedrera).

CASA CALVET *1898–1904*

Courtesy of AISA

THE house that Gaudí built for the Calvet family on Carrer de Casp in the center of Barcelona, a few blocks from the Passeig de Gracia, is the most reserved design in his entire career. It was conceived as a block of apartments, with the Calvet family apartment on the first floor and office spaces and smaller apartments above it. While it is his most conventional project, restricted by space and the family's requirements, it too contains stylistic innovations, puns, and subversions of form—not to mention subversions of planning permission. As he would do with the Casa Milà, Gaudí deliberately took the building above the city's height limitations. When the authorities complained, he threatened to simply slice it off at the official permitted height. The fact that the building was awarded an award for architectural excellence by the city probably contributed to the decision to allow it to stay.

The chief style in the façade is a restrained interpretation of baroque, but already some of the features that would take wing in Gaudí's later private homes—balconies, roofline—are becoming pronounced and starting to undulate. If the exterior is restrained to keep in line with its rather dowdy neighbors, the interior is lavish, with some of his finest furniture and décor that points towards the sumptuous interiors of the Casa Milà and Casa Batlló. If the façade is straitlaced, it also contains details that would become signatures in Gaudí's work, as well as a number of curiosities.

CASA CALVET

UPPER BALCONIES

Courtesy of AISA

LIKE many of his urban projects, the Casa Calvet is difficult to see as Gaudí would have intended, short of bombing the buildings opposite (something that actually happened; more of which later). Yet even though it is hemmed in, this actually serves to accentuate some of the features, and even heightens an effect he essayed and actually intended on the roof.

The most striking detail of the Calvet house is its balconies. These are metalwork and patterned symmetrically across the rough country stone façade, alternating in flat and trefoil designs, the latter built on a floorplan of three lobes or leaves. They are already beginning to morph towards the alarming animal forms of the Casa Batlló balconies. The appearance of three levels of balconies is coincidence, although Gaudí allowed himself a trio of saints—the patron saints of the Calvet family—in the uppermost floor, and, above them, the saints' insignias. Two miniature balconies, purely decorative (as is the twin gable that caused Gaudí so much trouble with the authorities), in fact disguise winches used to heft furniture up to the individual apartments. In among the formal undulations of the rooftop gabling, Gaudí included two crosses—although this is almost a private conceit, as the crosses can barely be seen, less still recognized, from below. Indeed, given the wealth of iconography and symbolism in the buildings Gaudí designed before and after this one project, the Calvet is remarkable for its lack of Gaudían embellishment on the exterior. It is entirely possible, however, that this was due to an external factor. From its earliest days, the project was the subject of complaint from the inhabitants of a nearby convent, so much so that Gaudí built a screen around the back of the building to obviate their complaints about intrusion on privacy. As he tended to elaborate his plans as he went along, the austere visage of the Casa Calvet may reflect its geographical circumstances, or simply the wishes of the Calvet family.

CASA CALVET

INTERIOR

Courtesy of AISA

IF Gaudí took a light hand to the exterior of the Casa Calvet, he went to town on the interior, lavishing more attention on its furniture than he had in even the Palau Güell. Yet even here, many of his familiar decorative themes, with the exception of flower motifs, are absent.

Elegant stone—in fact prefabricated to resemble granite—clads the stairs, rising around an extraordinarily elaborate metal and wood electric lift. Spirals abound in two and three dimensions, the first in patterned tilework, the latter in smoothed helical spiral columns and stone columnar ornaments.

Some of his finest wooden furniture—the triangular tripodal stool, the flowing art nouveau-inspired chairs and benches—as well as upholstered designs appeared in the Casa Calvet. Not that one would wish to be seated on the benches for too long a time; those ridges would prove very uncomfortable after the briefest of stays.

This interior has proved surprisingly durable: when an explosion in the house opposite blew in the lower windows and damaged some pieces of furniture, the constituent parts remained intact and workmen were able to reassemble them without any trouble.

Perhaps most remarkable of the pieces, however, is the fabulous asymmetrical art nouveau mirror (opposite), a slender, molten lozenge of glass mounted in curlicues and nautilus whorls of gold-painted wood, that seems from this distance in time to be looking forward to the elongated gold elephants of Salvador Dalí.

The interior of the Casa Calvet is perhaps the most feminine of all Gaudí's work. The mirror particularly seems almost determinedly feminine in both intended use and actual design, and ornate candle holders have been placed in the middle of the glass for close examination at night. The mirror's hanging angle (looking downwards) suggests an easier use for someone sitting below it and turned slightly to look at their reflection. There is no use of a mirror in cathedrals or convents.

CASA CALVET

EXTERIOR FEATURES

Courtesy of Arcaid

GAUDÍ may have restrained himself when designing the front of the Calvet house, but it is rich in small and even perverse detail. It is, like its interior, strangely feminine in appearance. Stone and metalwork repeat subtle flower and mushroom forms, and although there doesn't appear to be a snake or lizard in sight, something unusual is happening here. Metal leafwork in the ornate stone oriel, the stone "bay window" above the front door, suggests decay, something Gaudí would develop in the metalwork on the La Pedrera balconies and which he would take to extremes on the façade of the Sagrada Familia.

As well as designing the metal peepholes, Gaudí provided the plan for the extraordinarily elaborate doorknockers. When anyone uses these fearsome devices, a lever lifts a cross that then strikes the back of a bug that has been fashioned beneath it. The bug symbolizes both contamination and evil: both are crushed by the act of entering the house. The bug is also sitting on a field of four lines, which may be a reference to the Catalan flag, although this is so hidden as to be almost conceptual art.

There is one more factor of interest about the Casa Calvet: its reverse façade. Where it might have been expected to echo the front, the rear of the building is in fact noticeably different. The balconies are rounded and almost anatomical in shape, art nouveau patterns now resemble scales and, rather carelessly, someone appears to have allowed a couple of quadruped stone dinosaurs into the back garden.

This is entirely fanciful, for no one could have known what Gaudí would design for his first house on the Passeig de Gracia, but it is almost as though the Casa Batlló is hatching out of the back of the Casa Calvet.

CRYPT OF THE COLONIA GÜELL CHURCH *1898–1914*

Courtesy of AISA

THE church of the Colonia Güell estate in Santa
Coloma de Cervelló, north of Barcelona, was to have
been Gaudí's first truly monumental building, but
like so many other projects it was never completed.
He was only able to build the crypt before the
project was halted. Sketches remain that give an
inkling of what the finished church would have
looked like, and he himself told colleagues that this
was, in effect, a dry run for the Sagrada Familia.

As well as giving a foretaste of the spectacular
interior spaces of the Sagrada, the Colonia Güell
church was also to be an exercise in naturalism, using
tree shapes and raw rock formations. After the
commissioned homes and apartment/office blocks,
here Gaudí was given free rein to experiment with
his most imaginative ideas. Considering this, the
cancellation of the project must have been especially
galling, particularly after the nineteen years it took to
nurse the building this far.

Roughly contemporary with the Park Güell,
this was another of Gaudí and Güell's experiments in
social engineering. Where the Park offered a
romantic suburban idyll to Barcelona's rich, Güell's
project at Santa Coloma was a *colonia industrial*, a
workers' colony for the employees of Güell's textile
factory in the town. It was fashioned along the
lines of "philanthropist" workers' settlements such as
Port Sunlight and Bournville in Britain (Güell was
something of an Anglophile, and visited occasionally
on business). Most observers have read the project as
a genuinely progressive social experiment, although
Güell's critics point out that he was not averse to
employing child labor.

CRYPT OF THE COLONIA GÜELL CHURCH

FAÇADE/ENTRANCE

Courtesy of AISA

SURVIVING sketches for the completed Colonia church indicate something even more outlandish than the Sagrada Familia: a cluster of huge conical towers suggesting, in modern imagery, space rockets or even the swooping lines of a roller-coaster. If anything, it is similar to Gaudí's late, unrealized, Hotel project for Manhattan. What we see today, however, is simply the "basement" and the supports that would have hefted this fantastical structure up into the sky. In 2000, the crypt had to be closed for fundamental structural repairs. Its columns and load-bearing structures were meant to have a large, and heavy, building standing on them, and Gaudí had planned them and calculated their weight-bearing capacity with that in mind. Without the church on top, their structural integrity was dangerously compromised, and alterations had to be made to stop the crypt falling down.

As with the stonework elements in the Park Güell, Gaudí was looking to nature and landscape for inspiration. As in all of his landscaped projects, the crypt was assimilated into the terrain, almost absorbed by a gently sloping hill covered in pines. When the precise plot was decided, Gaudí noted that there was a mature pine tree where the steps into the building were meant to go. While others might simply have chopped the tree down, Gaudí took the staircase around it.

CRYPT OF THE COLONIA GÜELL CHURCH

INTERIOR

Courtesy of AISA

WHERE the effects of the Torre Bellesguard were to
involve a certain legerdemain with materials, here
Gaudí explicitly intended to expose the raw stone
and earth that formed the body of the church. As well
as brick—which Robert Hughes reads as a metaphor
for baked earth, or *la patria*, homeland—Gaudí
employed Garraf stone and that most primeval of
stones, basalt, in the columns. Each material has a
different load-bearing capacity: brick was used for
lighter loads, sometimes in near-circular brick shapes,
suggested heads of corn; the Garraf stone was
employed to support heavier loads; and the basalt to
support the heaviest, notably the central dome.

While the columns affect a tree-like or rough-
hewn appearance, they were in fact "carrying"
parabolic or helical forms concealed within their
shapes. As in other Gaudí cellar spaces, the
appearance is almost of a forest of randomly placed
columns. In fact, as he would essay in his work on
the renovation of the cathedral at Palma de Mallorca
and in the Sagrada Familia, the columns were
carefully distributed to allow the best views of the
altar from around the interior. Despite his arcane
symbolism, Gaudí never lost sight of the building's
primary function, and in fact he saw function, form,
and decoration as an inseparable trinity in his work.

CRYPT OF THE COLONIA GÜELL CHURCH

PORTICO

Courtesy of AISA

ROUGHLY contemporary with the Park Güell, the Colonia crypt benefited from innovations being made on the slopes of the bald mountain. Josep Marià Jujol applied his *trencadis* technique to the portico of the crypt and a series of stations of the cross near it. Where the *trencadis* mosaics of the Park were textured patterns or abstractions, here, as befitting the setting, the designs became more sedate, formal, and representational, although the color work is no less dazzling. As well as formal geometric shapes and plant/leaf emblems, they included that other Gaudí signature motif, the margallo or palmetto palm frond.

Jujol and Gaudí also incorporated a variety of religious shapes, including the lustrous blue primitive crosses, and bosses similar to those in the Hall of 100 Columns, although here featuring medieval cross shapes. For the keystone at the center of the portico, Jujol fashioned a pattern from a cross, a carpenter's saw, and an anagram of St Joseph's initials—a device that would appear in the Park and, later, on the spires and other features of the Sagrada Familia. Joseph is, of course, the patriarch of the sacred family. The columns here, as well as resembling rough-hewn stone, also see the emergence of an allusion either to vegetable matter or perhaps even the weave of the materials produced at the Colonia, a sly reference that would appear elsewhere in the Crypt.

Gaudí's use of vegetable imagery is perhaps another of his many signs of the mortality of man in comparison to the ubiquity of God. The obvious incongruity of what are very perishable items being hewn from stone seems no less unbelievable than so much of the Church's teachings. They could well be a symbol of Gaudí's personal coming to terms with the contradictions inherent in religion, as well, of course, as being reminders of the natural world which surrounds us, even in the midst of a stone city.

CRYPT OF THE COLONIA GÜELL CHURCH

WINDOWS

Courtesy of AISA

AS can be seen in the *trencadís* mosaics of
the Park, something approaching a subversion of
material and/or style is at work in this period of
Gaudí's career. This might, considering the readings
of the Park by Josep M. Carandell, be an allusion to
the transformational processes of alchemy. It might
also, in a simpler explanation and given Gaudí's
concerns with the integrity of materials and their
origin, merely be an elegant personal conceit, or
pun. Two such devices make their appearance in the
fabric of the Colonia crypt. Most of the windows are
stained and carry cross-like patterns, although one at
least alludes to the masonic icon of the divider. All of
them, along with the air vents, are covered with
grilles. Some are of an extremely fine metal, in fact
used weaving needles from Güell's textile factory.
Others resemble strips or folds of cloth, but are in
fact metalwork (which is where Robert Hughes sees
a link with the soft fabric sculptures of Claes
Oldenburg). For Gaudí, again, these were textual as
well as textural: incorporating the tools of the *colonia
industrial* into the fabric of the place of worship, and
using the metalwork in the crypt to quote the very
material that the worshippers produced in the
factory during the working week.

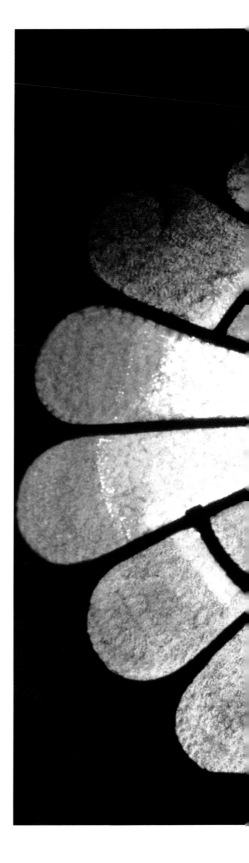

CRYPT OF THE COLONIA GÜELL CHURCH

CRYPT INTERIOR

Courtesy of AISA

IF, as seems likely, the Colonia's churchgoers had difficulty concentrating on the liturgy while inside this Stygian marvel, Gaudí devised a way to help them focus on their devotions. In some of the most exquisite furniture he ever designed, he produced molded seats that were explicitly intended to keep the congregation alert, perhaps even on the edge of their seats. As with the organic molding of the snake bench in the Park, the prayer benches were specially designed to keep the sitter erect and attentive. Or, perhaps, to test the allure of the church and the power of the priest to keep his congregation interested in the same old sermons. With Gaudí it is sometimes impossible to tell if he is testing God, himself or everyone else on their belief. These interiors are possible evidence of Gaudí's growing interest in the power of nature, of the existence of a very real threat to the idea of immortality offered by the church and absolute belief in God.

For the font at the rear of the chapel, Gaudí decided, for probably the first time in his career, to actually use a piece of raw nature, a giant clam-like shell, as itself rather than echoing it, copying it, or mediating it in any way. Held by three supports extending from a base of extravagant metalwork, and secured to one of the stone pillars, the font, meant to hold holy water, looks slightly impractical—but it also looks sublime. Is this Gaudí's great joke on God? In baptising the innocent child into the House of God, Gaudí had the priest immerse the baby in this very real and immense sea shell.

The use of the sea shell in paintings of mermaids and other creatures of the deep is a sign of the drowning power of sexual attraction—something that, apparently, Gaudí resisted his whole life, though not actually thoroughly (his one offer of marriage was rebuffed by a woman who then joined a convent). Gaudí's intended wife gave up her sex life—and in doing so his—for God.

CATHEDRAL OF PALMA DE MALLORCA *1889–1914*

Courtesy of the Institut Amatller d'Art Hispánic

IN 1899, Gaudí met Bishop Campins i Barceló of Palma de Mallorca when the bishop visited the site of the Sagrada Familia. A relatively young bishop, with progressive ideas about Church liturgy and architecture, Campins i Barceló was impressed by Gaudí's deep knowledge of both subjects. The bishop had plans to restore the Palma cathedral, and decided to ask Gaudí to take on the work. Despite his declared dislike for certain aspects of Gothic, Gaudí agreed.

Gaudí was by no means an absolutist in his dislike of Gothic features such as the flying buttress. He would alter the floorplan of the Sagrada, for example, in part to follow the floorplan of the mountainous Dom cathedral in Cologne, Germany, which certainly has buttresses to spare. Similarly, the Palma de Mallorca cathedral, looming over the Palma harbor just as the Dom looms over the Rhine, makes extravagant use of what Gaudí dismissed as a "crutch." If anything, Gaudí was on a mission to reform, or improve, Gothic.

In truth, Gaudí should have known better, especially after Astorga. While aesthetically sound, and liturgically watertight, his ideas fell foul of the chapter of the cathedral, the committee of priests who oversaw and rubber-stamped works on the building. Gaudí's aims were simple—to restore features that had been shifted over the centuries, and to improve the public's access to this space of worship—but the priests found his work too "modern."

CATHEDRAL OF PALMA DE MALLORCA

INTERIOR

Courtesy of the Institut Amatller d'Art Hispánic

IT is a sign of how serious and devoted Gaudí's approach to the Palma cathedral project was that he spent the best part of a year researching its history and cross-referencing that with liturgical texts. As a result, he uncovered a "lost" altar from the fourteenth century that had been covered by an eighteenth-century alteration to the cathedral. (This was confirmed by the head of the cathedral's archives, and perhaps rankled with the chapter.)

Gaudí's plans were relatively simple, although they did include some designs of his own which, true to form for him, alarmed the chapter. Throughout his career Gaudí seemed to make a point of breaking with traditions which underpinned aspects of the church, despite working within and for them for so long. If, as it seems it was, his own faith was constantly being tested he seemed determined to test the faith of the church in him and his abilities.

Within the Palma cathedral Gaudí moved the stalls for the choir closer to the altar, leaving the nave to be used by worshippers, an act of ecclesiastical democracy that he had pursued at the Colonia Güell and would repeat in the Sagrada. This had the effect of drastically altering the shape and lighting in the entire building, which was where he began to draw down the wrath of the chapter.

His own contributions to the building included a wall of iridescent glazed tiles at the back of the apse, true to his belief in the use of color and the importance of color to the liturgy. The chapter took a dim view of this innovation. He also insisted on using fragments of the Gospels, as he had used religious texts elsewhere in his works, which the chapter also disliked. History would prove Gaudí right, but not even the bishop could sway his reactionary colleagues.

CATHEDRAL OF PALMA DE MALLORCA

ROSE WINDOW

Courtesy of the Institut Amatller d'Art Hispánic

IF one may question aspects of Gaudí's philosophy, such as his self-confessed arrogance and political naïveté, one cannot doubt for a second his career-long devotion to bringing beauty, we might even say a transcendent beauty, to public, domestic, and religious spaces. In the Palma cathedral restoration, he even broke one of his cardinal rules about ecclesiastical architecture—he abhorred the floodlighting of churches and cathedrals, and insisted that only real candles, never electric, should be placed on altars—to bring light and a sense of wonder.

He replaced the original square canopy above the altar with a new, seven-sided canopy, replete with symbolism of the Holy Spirit, Pentecost, the Crucifixion, Mary, and St John. These he illuminated with clusters of tiny electric bulbs, replacing the glare of ordinary bulbs with a misty haze of light resembling a celestial galaxy or nebula. Before he abandoned work in the face of the chapter's intransigence, he also managed to reopen two previously blocked windows, illuminating them with his own technique of creating stained glass from various layers of primary colors.

Gaudí's plans for the cathedral were drastic compared to the patchwork of changes that had occurred over the centuries but, as the archivist's research into the provenance of the fourteenth-century altar proved, essentially sound. His disappointment with the chapter's reaction was probably the factor that determined him, in 1914, to abandon all other projects to concentrate on the Sagrada Familia for what would be the rest of his life.

PARK GÜELL *1900–14*

NO one should approach the Park Güell, either in person or in print, without preparing themselves for the experience. There is nothing else in Europe—from the whimsical Mediterraneanisms of Portmeirion to the fairy-tale castles Leo von Klenze built for Ludwig I of Bavaria—to compare with this orgy of imagination and symbolism run amok over the foothills of the Tibidabo mountain.

In hindsight, the hippies Robert Hughes describes taking drugs to better appreciate Gaudí's fantastical failed housing estate were probably closer to understanding its spirit than we might imagine. Magic mushrooms are in fact among the first things you see when you arrive at the Park.

Mischievous simile does the Park Güell a disservice, for it has a deeply serious intellectual agenda at its core, but it remains utterly stunning that two sober, conservative, middle-aged Catholics such as Gaudí and Eusebi Güell should embark on such a project.

It is a measure of the dynamic of industrialized nineteenth-century Barcelona that its richer families, such as Güell's, were able to purchase entire mountains on its outskirts. Yet it seems unlikely that any other family would have built a dormitory theme park whose symbolism invites description in the terminology of dementia.

There is so much at work in the Park Güell, including what some have interpreted as occult symbolism, that approached as a whole the Park induces sensory overload. Not even Umberto Eco's theory of hyper-reality can begin to explain just what is happening here—nor, indeed, what Antoni Gaudí i Cornet and Eusebi Güell i Bacigalupi intended in this semiotic whirlwind.

PARK GÜELL

ENTRANCE

Courtesy of Richard Bryant / Arcaid

WHEN Güell first purchased the Muntanya Pelada and he and Gaudí set about designing their utopian community, the landscape around it was still open countryside. The Güell family already owned a sizeable mansion on the edge of the property—it is now a school, separated from the Park by fences—but contemporary photographs show horse-drawn carriages approaching the Park entrance across fields. Like a number of other Gaudí projects on the perimeter of Barcelona, the city has crept up on it in the intervening decades.

The Park would have the most extensive symbolic program of any of Gaudí's secular works. Modern visitors may see the Park as little more than a colorful folly, but Gaudí and Güell wanted it to reflect a complex system of references to Catalan myth, religious symbolism, and improving philosophy borrowed from Bishop Torras i Bagès, a key ideologue of the turn-of-the-century Catalan renaissance. This symbolism would influence the slightest details in the project, from the positioning of its various features down to the choice of materials for the *trencadis* mosaics and even the flora distributed about the grounds.

As in the case of the prospective buyers who showed interest in the Park only to be put off by the interview process, it is likely that Gaudí and Güell's intended symbolism went straight over the heads of most visitors. The difference between what Gaudí intended and what the public read could be seen as a measure of the distance between opinion on the Catholic right and opinion on the streets of Barcelona. Certainly, history would be unambiguous in its opinion.

After the Sagrada Familia, the Park is probably the most important Gaudí site on the tourist trail in Barcelona, but few visitors are aware of the intense intellectual message Gaudí wanted his Park to impart.

PARK GÜELL

GATES

Courtesy of Ken Walsh/Bridgeman Art Library

THE name—whose appearance in cartoon-like cigar-band logos on the exterior walls has been interpreted as a reference to Eusebi Güell's considerable interests in the Cuban tobacco industry—gives us the first clue about the Park Güell. It is named "Park" and not the Catalan "Parc" (although the construction remains Spanish: noun before name), because Güell intended the project to be his version of the "garden cities" springing up in England at the end of the nineteenth century. (True, you don't find this sort of architecture in Welwyn Garden or Hampstead, but Gaudí and Güell were both aficionados of the ruralism of Englishmen John Ruskin and William Morris.)

The project, planned as an estate of some 60 individual houses on a 50-acre plot distributed around Muntanya Pelada, "Bald Mountain," to the north-west of the city, has been read as a "utopian" settlement built around grand communal areas. The fact that only one plot was sold suggests that Gaudí and Güell perhaps set their sights a little too high: people did apply to purchase plots, but either failed the stringent interview process involved or were put off by it. It seems that Gaudí and Güell didn't want just any old Catalan in their utopia.

The project was built (and today is still) beyond the reach of Barcelona's public transport system, inspiring its one valiant homesteader, lawyer Martín Trías Domènech, to suggest, rather heretically, that the tram that did for Gaudí in 1926 was getting its own back for this slight. Some have suggested that the Park's distance from the center and the interview process may have been specifically designed to exclude rather than include. The symbolism that starts to unfold at the entrance gates may tell us why.

PARK GÜELL

ROOF DECORATIONS

Courtesy of Richard Bryant/Arcaid

THE Park Güell bursts with so much invention that it is difficult to know where to start describing its splendors. If the cigar-band medallions for the name have inaugurated a sign hunt in the park, before we are inside there are allusions to masonic iconography that will recur across the landscape. On the façade of the left-hand pavilion to the gate, the inscription *Alaba por*—"praise for"—has been read as an anagram containing coded references to the masonic lodge. Indeed, the visitor is about to walk between two lodges.

The shapes in both lodges are melting into echoes of trees and trunks, teeth, skulls, sockets, scales, and carapaces. The leprous red mushrooms on the chimneys are *amanita muscaria*, fly agaric, and refer to Güell's hobby of mycology, mushroom hunting. Gaudí is probably innocent of any allusions to the poisonous agaric's reputation as a psychotropic drug, either in its erotic form, as Spanish fly, or psychedelic, as the magic mushroom. (But, but: at least one Gaudí expert believes he may have experimented with *amanita muscaria* to test its visionary potential.) There is a theory that the blue and white tower, employing the colors of the coat of arms of the Comillas family (friends and clients of Gaudí), is the trunk of an elephant whose four limbs form the rock "garage"—now the entrance to a visitors' bathroom—opposite. (The elephant, if he or she is such a thing, would later amble down the Passeig de Gracia to pose as model for the columns outside the Casa Milà.)

The technical innovation that first becomes apparent on entering this funfair with no rides is the decoration on the roofs of the lodges. Gaudí had already begun using abstract and purely geometric shapes to decorate buildings, notably on the roof of El Capricho, but here, like the architectonic features of wall, roof, window, and door, the shapes begin to dissolve. Among the chief innovations, recognized by critics such as Robert Hughes and Josep M. Carandell, is Gaudí's single-handed "invention" of collage, some time before Matisse's snail or the Dadaists' incorporation of found materials in their art.

PARK GÜELL

MOSAIC DESIGNS

Courtesy of Richard Bryant / Arcaid

WHILE Gaudí's ideas can still seem avant-garde to this day, it is unlikely that he read them this way: what we see as radical aesthetic innovations he saw as simple efforts to improve pattern, color, and sheen, borrowing ideas from nature. In fact, as a major feature of the Park would show, he considered ancient Greece to be his major influence here, in particular his belief—later proved correct—that the Greeks painted their stonework.

Gaudí's collaboration on the Park's *trencadis* designs with Jujol—who would become a lauded architect in his own right—flows from the roofs of the pavilions, up the double stairway, and on to the bench that snakes around the plaza above. Some have read heraldic, and hence Catalanist, axes and knives in the roofs, and in the routes the fragments take as they flow down from the roofs. Here, the most remarkable thing starts to happen. Heraldic allusions and heroic bosses shatter into fragments that reassemble in shocking new forms on the balustrades of the steps and the most famous feature of the Park, the snake bench.

PARK GÜELL

MOSAIC DETAIL

Courtesy of Richard Bryant/Arcaid

THE intervening decades since the design of the Park Güell have seen the emergence of several schools of art that seem to echo ideas found in Gaudí's work, not least the *trencadis* designs of the Park. We should pause before reading causality between the two. It is indeed possible that the young Joan Miró and Pablo Picasso both took some inspiration from Gaudí. However, given the disapproval that dogged his works from the end of the *modernista* period (critics tend to date its death around 1910) right up until the 1980s, it is unlikely that Gaudí had much influence over the several eruptions of modernism in northern Europe. He was pre-empting the ideas of revolutionaries, however, from the cubists of 1920s Paris to the postmodernists of 1990s Manhattan.

Even in the twenty-first century, what Gaudí was doing with line, color, and form can be seen as radical. The mosaic patterns displayed could easily be the work of a modern-day artist determined to shock. The patterns are both surreal and easily digestible. They can cause no offence to anyone at a casual glance. The most remarkable thing about them, of course, is that they exist at all and have done for so long. There is function in this form but it is also extremely fanciful. As if bored of austerity, Gaudí's detail here is not reflective of God nor in praise of Him. It is strangely natural, reflecting the blue of the sky and enhancing the green of the grass. Clearly the work of man and oddly fragile-seeming, the mosaic is both a tribute to the work of the Ancients and a mockery of the same; the Romans made mosaics to reflect life and glorify their gods. Gaudí's work is pure, unadulterated, unexplained art. In the open. Free.

PARK GÜELL

PARK ROOFSCAPE

Courtesy of Richard Bryant/Arcaid

GAUDÍ waved goodbye to the conventional roof from the parapets of the Park Güell. Here, on either side of the entrance, the slumbering stegosaurus is waking.

If some critics are to be believed, the stegosaurus is also embarking on a crash course in Catalanist semiotics. The red and white on the exterior of the park are, apparently, the colors of the ancient Phoenician fleet, probably the region's earliest settlers and thus the founders of the Catalan gene pool. The blue and white of the southern pavilion's tower, elephant trunk or no, refers not only to the Comillas family banner but also to the coat of arms of the counts of Montcada, who launched medieval Catalonia's invasion of Mallorca, a key event in Catalan myth-history. The colors also allude to the Bavarian court, further linking park and owner to the glorious Catalan past.

Less crazily, the Park Güell represents the full flowering of Gaudí's use of the *trencadis* collage technique, although he would finesse this technique in one further and quite literally illuminating way in his plans for the Sagrada Familia. The credit for the Park's *trencadis* decorations must go as much to Gaudí's assistant Josep Marià Jujol as to Gaudí.

The curved battlement of the roof is another strangely feminine statement by Gaudí. Although one can see the almost defensive qualities and echoes of the warring past of the city in their position, these shapes are female in form. There are none of the forbidding sharp edges or spikes of earlier work. There are no cutting edges here, only soft, voluptuous rolls that speak softly to the sky.

Even the wide-mouthed mock gargoyles beneath the rolling edges fail to impose a frightening edge to the roof.

PARK GÜELL

STAIRS TO THE PLAZA

Courtesy of AISA

IT is easy to overlook just what is going on here on the steps of the Park. As well as the symbolism in the figures on the stairs, and the allusion to mythological epic in encountering and safely passing the guardian lizard, there is symbolism at work in the entire color scheme. The visitor has to stop and do a double-take. At first, the décor appears to be domestic glazed ceramic tile, haphazardly smashed and reapplied in the mosaic equivalent of crazy paving. Yet, like an infinitesimal library from a Jorge Luis Borges story, the *trencadis* designs of the Park Güell present an encyclopedic stylebook ranging as far back as pre-Christian Arabic design and as far forward as the crockery art of Julian Schnabel and even the dot paintings of Damien Hirst.

Again, this should not necessarily be read as Gaudí's specific intention: he certainly wasn't in the prediction business, and would have hated most of late-twentieth-century art. The provenance of the Park's *trencadis* mosaics is almost comically prosaic: Gaudí and Jujol asked their workmen to bring any old tiling or porcelain to the site for inclusion in the designs. Jujol himself contributed a particularly loathed dinner set, featuring cherubs disporting themselves among little fluffy clouds still visible in the design. A newspaper article contemporary to the project even reported the writer's bemusement at the sight of Gaudí's workmen enthusiastically smashing stuff up only for it to be incorporated into the building work.

PARK GÜELL

SALAMANDER FOUNTAIN

Courtesy of AISA

SOME have read further references to the tethered dragon protecting the Garden of the Hesperides in the lizard straddling the fountain on the Park's steps. Others see a crocodile, and still more the salamander, traditionally the pet of choice for the medieval alchemist and a likely reference to Güell's time spent in Nîmes, home of the Place de la Salamandre. The gecko-like toes gripping the bathtub edges of the fountain seem to vote for the harmless if symbolically loaded salamander. If anything, its pose is the defensive stillness of the lizard hoping to camouflage itself in its surroundings (it would be too anthropomorphic to read that rictus as a smile). Brilliantly colored like a central American, perhaps Mayan, artefact, the salamander is just one member of an ensemble performing on the Park's monumental stairway.

Below it is another fountain, issuing from the mouth of that most Gaudían of reptiles, the snake, whose head protrudes from a heraldic shield featuring the red and yellow bars of the Catalan flag—Wilfred the Hairy's blood come back to haunt us. Below that, in an eldritch grotto of rock and moss, masonic icons such as the compass and divider have insinuated themselves into the tiny caves. These in turn recall the grottoes of the Ciutadella fountain, thought to be Gaudí's work. Above them all, a hooded bench like the aperture of a Greek tragedian mask completes the set. The effect is ouroboros-like, as though each descending stage is about to devour the next. There is a final symbolic flourish in the *trencadís* model of a tripod—more arcane and possibly Masonic imagery—that Josep M. Carandell also reads as an omphalos, the mythical navel of the world.

PARK GÜELL

HALL OF 100 COLUMNS

Courtesy of AISA

THE calmest spot, literally and figuratively, in the Park Güell is its agora, the marketplace that formed the focus of the ancient Greek town. The stairs lead up to a "hypostyle" hall that is constructed of columns, here Doric in style, which Gaudí designed as a meeting place and one where merchants would sell their wares.

The so-called "Hall of 100 Columns" has its own secrets to impart, not least that there are in fact only 86 of them. Gaudí left out the other fourteen to introduce air into the space and avoid clutter. Gaudí also had another trick up his sleeve.

Muntanya Pelada was bare, scrubby rock when Güell bought it, with no natural water. As the Park had been designed as a miniature Olympian village, water was vital to making it work. Gaudí turned the engineering skills that had designed the Ciutadella park fountain tank to the problem of collecting the Park's rainwater as it tumbled down the mountain. As before, he was particularly concerned that his design should work in harmony with the landscape. Thus, all structures, roads, and paths snake around its contours.

The contours of the mountain would also send most of its rainfall down towards the entrance, so the sand-floored plaza above the Hall filters rainwater into runaways that flow into pipes inside the columns and down into a vast hidden tank that feeds the fountains and waters the surrounding gardens and beds.

Even though it is off-limits to visitors, sculptural features have appeared here too, not least a ship's prow cleaving the waters when the tank, which can hold thousands of gallons of water, fills up. As with much of Gaudí's work, that which is unseen by the human eye is clearly visible to omnipotent beings. It is almost as if he is hedging his bets as to which Being that might be, with his paganistic references and embellishments, none of which are so obvious as to suggest that the man does not worship a Christian God.

PARK GÜELL

HALL CEILING DESIGNS

Courtesy of AISA

THE authorship of the designs on the Hall roof is disputed, but the collaborative architectural process, especially in the work of Gaudí and Jujol in the Park, should be credited to both men equally. It too lends itself to Josep Carandell's thesis that vibrant occult symbolism is alive throughout the Park. (It is, however, both curious and remarkable that Carandell omits any such interpretation from his readings of similar images when they appear in the Sagrada Familia.)

The *trencadis* designs on the Hall roof are among the most exquisite in Gaudí and Jujol's work, and the most accessible to the visitor (the others being high in the structure of the Sagrada, or on the Palau Güell roof). They describe a solar and planetary calendar, with the sun and moon represented in their quarterly cycles. Snake shapes, some of them three-dimensional, recur, as do lizard heads, octopuses and, curiously, a child's doll. All of these are in relief. It is possible that these symbols have faintly pagan undertones, or at least a Christian-pantheist subtext.

Josep Carendell has read allusions to the turn-of-the-century mystical religious sect Rosicrucianism, here. This is something that would also recur later in the symbolism in the Park, in the mysterious Calvary shrine placed on a small hill in a far corner of the Park. Carandell also detects numerology at work in the space, indeed the entire Park, and mythical references besides.

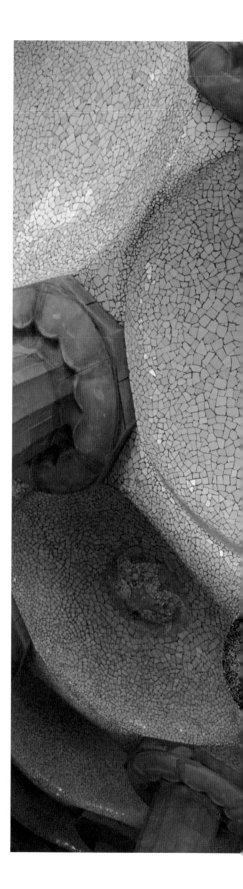

PARK GÜELL

SNAKE BENCH

Courtesy of AISA

THERE are also coded messages in the visitors' favorite feature of the Park Güell, the "snake" bench. Gaudí's innovative work with *trencadis* mosaics reached its peak with this design, although the effect has been diminished over the decades by wear, tear, and unscrupulous hands prying mementos of their visit from the fabric of the bench.

Gaudí intended the entire Park to be a theater, with the plaza as its stage, and indeed plays and other performances were staged here. As well as continuing with the obvious—here almost throwaway—snake references, the wavy design of the bench also optimizes space in a way suggesting theatrical boxes (or like a stone equivalent of diner banquette seating). The bench is molded to the human form; one legend claims that Gaudí seated a naked workman in a mold and repeated the impression throughout the bench. (It is most definitely not, however, a kissing seat; the conservative Gaudí was mortified to learn that courting couples used his Park for their assignations.)

As well as the brilliantly colored mosaic work, the bench conceals fragments of text, in Catalan and Latin. The bench had been *in situ* for around fifty years before these secret messages were discovered in the interstices of the *trencadis*. Some have detected a dialogue between the Virgin Mary and a petitioner, with their fragmentary comments flowing in different directions along the bench. The script is in a clumsy hand, although here too there may be artifice, an attempt to obscure the author's (or authors') identity. Today they bring to mind the artist Tom Phillips's work with subliminal texts, allowing fragments to rise at random into the foreground of the work.

PARK GÜELL

SNAKE BENCH DESIGNS

Courtesy of AISA

THE various uses of *trencadis* mosaics in the Park also have a further, deeper, function. While we can trace a line from pre-Christian Moorish designs to others that can seem shockingly modern, Gaudí and Jujol were pursuing a subtle religious symbolism in their use of color. Conrad Kent and Dennis Prindle, in their architectural study *Park Güell*, detect repetitions, rhythms, and patterns of color throughout the Park and even beyond. Yellow, green, and blue are by far the most dominant colors, as for Gaudí they represented the virtues of Faith, Hope, and Charity.

More conventional color symbolism is also at work on the bench and throughout the Park: white for purity, black for mourning, and purple for piety or penitence (a very Gaudían theme). Stars and moons also recur in the system, as do flowers representing the Holy Trinity (fleurs-de-lis) and the Virgin Mary (the rose).

As Kent and Prindle point out, by the time Gaudí and Jujol came to start work on the snake bench, the nature of the Park had changed irrevocably. Not only was no one interested in buying the building plots there, but following the bloody events of the Setmana Tragica in 1909—when Gaudí watched from the Park as his Sagrada Familia burned—the religious establishment was retreating from social intervention into a more withdrawn, metaphysical spirituality. The Setmana Tragica, or "Tragic Week," in which 100 people died, was a workers' uprising that transformed into an orgy of anticlerical violence during which religious properties were burned and clerical cemeteries even sacked. Gaudí dedicated himself to a variety of causes designed to repair the rift between Church and populace through art. Thus he deliberately used the Park, as he would the Sagrada Familia, as a didactic device. According to Kent and Prindle, a journey through the Park's color scheme was intended as nothing less than a journey to Paradise.

PARK GÜELL

TRENCADIS DETAILS

Courtesy of AISA

MORE Gaudían legerdemain can be seen in the detailing of the *trencadis* mosaics on the stairs. The concavities in the square tile details, which would recur in the details of the Sagrada Familia, smuggle circular shapes into the squares, hinting at more alchemical change. As well as quoting a wealth of pictorial sources, which could be traced back to Roman and Greek art as well as Moorish, there are games of alteration and subversion of form at work here. Dismantling, erasure, and displacement are ideas that were still current for young Spanish architects such as Enric Miralles up until the end of the 20th century and beyond. Here, in Gaudí's Park, these ideas are displayed in two ways. Firstly, conventional tiles, with Moorish, floral, geometric or art nouveau patterns, are broken up and reassembled into abstractions and shattered forms that would later recur in cubism, vorticism, and other modernist subversions of nature. (A generally accepted theory is that Picasso, who would have seen Gaudí's *trencadis* mosaics during his years living in Barcelona, did indeed take some of the architect's ideas with him when he departed conventional representation for the disjointed planes of cubism.) Secondly, some of the tiles, notably those featuring precise rows of pink dots and geometric patterns, were placed in the *trencadis* mosaics to resemble broken yet badly "fixed" versions of themselves. Breakage, alteration, forgery, and the undermining of the original artist or author would all become key devices of postmodernism, although such structuralist games were not the aim of the great nature-lover Gaudí. His attentions were focused elsewhere; in the middle of the steps, where he unleashes more monsters on the Park's hapless visitors.

PARK GÜELL

LANDSCAPE

Courtesy of AISA

ALTHOUGH it would be reified, or perhaps reinvented, in the structures Gaudí imposed on the bald mountain, actual nature takes a back seat to art in the Park Güell. The passage of time, mismanagement, deliberate vandalism and, ironically, Mother Nature herself have all subtly and not so subtly altered the living landscape. Cypress, palms, planes, and other trees are indigenous to the region, as are aloe, datura, broom, and rhododendron. So too are the herbs, such as rosemary and thyme, that appear in the Park. But much of the undeveloped land here is just brush and wild growth that has developed over the decades (and which has been damaged by the incursions of foraging visitors). Although nature itself has overrun Gaudí's original intentions for the plants and trees to be featured in the Park, Kent and Prindle read a symbolism in the native flora he wanted planted here. As with his use of symbolism in other projects, such as the living landscape he envisaged for the façade of the Casa Milà, these flora would enhance the religious and cultural ideals that he saw embodied in the Park.

Gaudí's relationship with landscape was a curious one. He clearly believed that his buildings should exist in harmony with it—as when the Güell Crypt merges into the hillside—and that the material of his buildings should echo that harmony—as in the material quarried and used here in the Park. But with the exception of Park Güell, and the garden of El Capricho, he made few sorties into landscaping itself. Landscape reverberates through his buildings, and most of them were, of course, urban structures, but it is almost as though he had an ambiguous attitude to the great outdoors, except when he was copying it in stone.

PARK GÜELL

STONEWORK

Courtesy of AISA

BEFORE visitors reached Paradise in Gaudí and Güell's scheme of things, they had to pass through Alton Towers. This was not, of course, the modern-day Alton Towers of Corkscrew roller-coasters and Black Hole dark rides, but the Victorian mansion, its park and numerous glades and follies, which Güell knew from visits to England. Park Güell was a variant on the immensely popular "anthology parks" that were opening all over northern Europe. These promised visitors the opportunity to visit numerous exotic landscapes—mountains, lakes, jungles, and so on—within the safety and comfort of a manicured park.

The "theme" to Gaudí and Güell's theme park was not a flip or frivolous one that modern-day habitués of theme parks know and adore, of course. For them the theme was nothing less than personal salvation. For both men, the Park was inextricably linked with Montserrat, the mountaintop shrine to the north of Barcelona. Linked to Barcelona by a new train line, Montserrat became a hugely popular destination for excursions and religious pilgrimages, which were themselves a key form of recreation during this period.

The mountain held a special meaning for Catalans. It had been a refuge at various crucial points in Catalan legend, and in the 1900s Christian geologists were actually trying to link it to the biblical creation story. Indeed, Kent and Prindle report that Güell was keen that archeological finds unearthed in the park be used by Christian authorities to help refute Darwinism (*The Origin of Species* had been published in 1859). This may seem a forlorn hope in hindsight, but Gaudí and Güell felt themselves engaged in a battle for the souls of mankind, or at least those residing in Barcelona.

PARK GÜELL

WAVE PORTICO

Courtesy of AISA

ARCHITECTURE, in Schelling's famous phrase, is "frozen music." Here, in Gaudí's stone portico above the plaza, it begins to resemble frozen weather. In a dazzling, if symbolically puzzling, feat of engineering Gaudí fashioned what looks like the "tube" of a breaking wave into the bald mountainside. What further look like frozen waterspouts, or whirlpools (some see champagne glasses), support the breaking wave. Gaudí seems to have studied the mechanics of waves—again, taking a lesson from his "first teacher," nature—in constructing this feature of the park. The structure and its supports are perfectly designed to handle stress and distribute weight in the wave, as later calculations using computer programs would prove. Josep Carandell sees the wave as the Red Sea parting to allow the Children of Israel to flee Egypt. It is possible that the nature-loving Gaudí would have seen this form in photographs of spectacular erosion effects, such as the Wave Rock at Hyden in Australia.

PARK GÜELL

STONE SCULPTURES

Courtesy of AISA

TRUE to his philosophy of using the materials of the site to build on it, Gaudí employed rock quarried from the bald mountain to construct parts of the Park. The first we note is the holding wall at the rear of the theater plaza. The lower sections are built to resemble prehistoric monumental architecture—something we might stumble across at Chichen-Itza or Uxmal in the Yucatán, perhaps. Above, however, the stone is dissolving back into nature, suggesting the branches of a gymnosperm or palm—precisely what the structure was built to support above it. This harks back to the double allusions in the Güell Crypt, where materials from the site—weaving needles—were incorporated into metalwork for the windows, and where metalwork for the windows was also made to allude to the materials produced at the site. Here, Gaudí effects a witty echo between the stonework and the trees above.

However, after the exquisite handiwork of the *trencadis*, this is deliberately crude, rough-hewn stonework, suggesting textual as well as textural intent in Gaudí's designs. There is also symbolism at work: *La Lavanderia*, the stone washerwoman holding a basket on her head, has been read as a neophyte woman mason in the act of initiation into the lodge. Exactly why the architect would suggest the initiation of a woman into a strictly male dominion is, as with much of his private life, unclear. As previously stated, Gaudí's relationship with the opposite sex was far from "normal" and there is little evidence of his ever enjoying a close or long relationship with a woman. Whether this somewhat indistinct feminine shape is a statement on the position of women in society—one that is strongly male dominated—or whether it is merely a fanciful notion of Gaudí's is impossible to tell.

More usual Gaudí signatures can be found in the grottoes, niches, and a secret chapel which are now hidden from public view and which suggest some religious imagery at play.

PARK GÜELL

GAUDÍ HOUSE

Courtesy of Richard Bryant/Arcaid

THE curious stone globes leading away from the plaza, in fact a rosary that Gaudí is said to have walked regularly, stopping to pray at each station, leads along the top of the monumental stone work towards the Gaudí house, now a museum. Along with the Güell family, whose house is now a public school next to the entrance, and Señor Trias's house near the peak of the mountain, Gaudí's house was one of only three completed on the site.

Gaudí moved into the house in 1906 with his father, his niece Rosita and a servant. This would not be a happy period: his father was ailing, and Rosita was becoming addicted to an alcoholic patent medicine that would precipitate a fatal heart attack a few years later. Gaudí was 55 years of age and had produced no heir to his family name. His personal life proved to be a series of tests of faith, both in himself and, it could be argued, in God, too. While so much of his work demonstrates a struggle against the way things are and how they could be, with the natural melding into the modern and man-made, with his strong non-secular works standing alongside pagan or almost mythic figures, his home life seems to have been more staid and conventional. But then, clearly, it had to be. He was *de facto* the head of the family and responsible for his father and sister. As difficult as it may have been, Gaudí had familial duties to perform.

By now, also, it was becoming clear that Güell's planned utopia was a failure. Güell died in 1918, and in 1923 the Park was sold to the authorities. Perhaps because the Gaudí house was designed by his assistant Francesc Berenguer, it has certain Gaudían touches about it, notably the *trencadis* chimney, the striking metalwork portico and interior balcony, and other individual features, but is otherwise unremarkable. It is almost as if Gaudí wanted the house he lived in to reflect his conformist position on home and family.

Today it is a museum and among the many delights of its interior are pieces of original furniture, some of which Gaudí designed himself.

PARK GÜELL

CALVARY

Courtesy of Richard Bryant / Arcaid

ONE of the most curious sights in the Park Güell is hidden in the south-western corner. On top of a smaller hill next to the bald mountain, Gaudí built a mysterious monument, and one laden with explicit, if ambiguous, symbolism. The hill, Turo de les Menes, or Iron Ore Hill, had once been mined for that substance. Here, Gaudí constructed a sealed stone structure with no visible entrance. The mound, with two flights of steps mounting it, resembles a talaiot, the mysterious prehistoric stone structures to be found in the countryside of Mallorca and Menorca. On top, Gaudí fashioned two crosses, one small, one tall, and a low truncated arrow. When viewed from a particular angle, all three line up, fusing into one symbol that displays both arrow and cross shapes.

Pointing out that the talaiot structure is lobed, or rose-shaped, Josep Carandell believes that there is a complex program of Catholic–masonic and even Rosicrucian imagery at work in this monument. Its appearance on this particular spot, with imposing views (certainly the best in the Park) down to city, sea, and the Montjuic mountain to the west, does lend itself to the suggestion that there is powerful imagery intended in the monument. In *fin-de-siècle* Europe, Rosicrucianism was just one alternative philosophy among dozens, such as Theosophy, popular among the middle-class intelligentsia. Rosicrucianism claimed special knowledge and powers from nature, including the transforming power of alchemy. It might not sit well with the petitions for Gaudí's beatification now with the Vatican, but there was even a Catholic version of the cult of the rosy cross. Given the preponderance of nature, animal, and vegetable symbols in the Park, it is not difficult to imagine Gaudí intending them to have a philosophical, even religious, meaning.

PARK GÜELL

HELICAL COLUMNS

Courtesy of Richard Bryant / Arcaid

GAUDÍ'S intuitive sense of structural integrity—along with his ability to hammer out the maths—is most evident in the helical columns he designed to support the upper walkway above the Park's plaza. Working with the bald mountain's rock, he fashioned—or rather forged—roughly dressed helical spiral columns and then canted them at a wild angle to absorb weight and pressure. Supporting plant beds and rough-hewn stone balconies, the columns fuse his use of the helix, in which the square is made to spiral into a cylindrical columnar shape, with more allusions to alchemy and weather. Here we see the first hints of the helical spirals that Joan Bergós would detect in later projects, notably the fire and whirlwind shapes in the chimneys of the Casas Batlló and Milà. These shapes could in fact be rock thermals.

Unfortunately, time, fashion, the materials themselves and, ironically, the weather have all had an adverse effect on this feature of the Park. During the decades when Gaudí's work lay ignored and largely untended, much of this stonework was damaged by erosion and simple wear and tear. While the spiral supports themselves remain intact, some of the upper balconies have begun to crumble and even fall apart. If the Park had been completed and maintained as Gaudí had originally intended, it is probable that much and perhaps all of this damage could have been averted. Renovation work in recent decades, which continues to this day, has restored the balconies to the state envisaged by Gaudí.

TORRE BELLESGUARD *1900–2*

Courtesy of Oronoz

THE Torre Bellesguard, built for the widow of an admirer of Gaudí's work, doña Maria Sagués, is something of an anomaly. It is one of Gaudí's later buildings, and part of what we might call his "Barcelona group," although it is remote from the center of Barcelona, and from the style of his other buildings in the city. Today it sits in the shadow of Norman Foster's startling javelin communications tower, just below the Tibidabo hill. (It is also the most frustrating for the visitor; a private property ringed by a very tall wall that obscures all but the upper part of the tower.) It is also worth noting that, while the building does indeed center on a tower, "torre" in Catalan was taken to mean a second, usually country, home.

Despite its period and situation, it turns away from the styles Gaudí was using at this time and heads back towards the neo-medievalism of his northern palaces. The Torre Bellesguard was, in many senses, his most patriotically Catalan project. The reasons for this are in the very soil on which it is built.

Doña Sagués' home was built on the site—indeed, ruins—of a summer home built in the fifteenth century by the count-king Martí I the Humane, the last of the count-kings of medieval Catalonia, and revered as a force for good in Barcelona and Catalonia. (Well, as much as medieval royalty could be.) Martí I built his summer home here high in the hills above the city because of the *bell esguard*—the "good view" of city, port, and sea. Doña Sagués' house would be nothing less than a time machine calibrated to take its owner and visitors back to the court of the Catalonian king.

TORRE BELLESGUARD

GATE

Courtesy of Oronoz

THE gate guarding the Torre Bellesguard entrance is the first hint of a fairly recondite theme running through the property: recondite not least because little of the property is on view from outside its tall perimeter walls. The art nouveau metalwork curlicues that flexed into and out of barbs and reptile stings in earlier metalwork designs here morph into the shapes of fishermen's barbel hooks, in a symbolism so complicated it could be read as code.

The entrance opens on to the grounds of Martí the Humane's summer home. The doorway to the house is flanked by two mosaic benches both featuring a shark, *tiburon,* beneath four red bars—the stripes of the Catalan flag, stained by Wilfred the Hairy's blood, here appearing in Gaudí's work in full Technicolor, as it were—superimposed with a golden M, a pun on both the owner's name and the Virgin Mary.

The entire symbolic ensemble is a reference to the medieval Catalan count-kings' supremacy over the western Mediterranean seas, a supremacy that reached its peak under Martí I the Humane. Little surprise, then, that Gaudí's gate enclosing this little bubble of Catalan history should be defended by the grappling bars of Martí's fleet.

TORRE BELLESGUARD

INTERIOR

Courtesy of Oronoz

TWO and possibly more contrary architectural styles are at work in the Torre Bellesguard. While its exterior aspires to a romantic neo-medievalism, the interior is altogether softer, suggesting a smoother version of the Arabic and Mudéjar styles of earlier buildings such as the Casa Vicens and El Capricho. With the signature arches banished to the attic space, where they are employed to support that dramatic northern Gothic roof, the domestic spaces on lower floors are plastered and painted a glowing creamy white. Mudéjar arches and domes are distributed throughout the public rooms and distribution spaces for solely decorative effect, and seem to be bulging out into almost organic extrusions, as though in sympathy with the building's contemporary and near-neighbor, the Park Güell.

The interior and exterior of the Torre Bellesguard are as different from each other as the interior and exterior of the pearl oyster, and this may in fact have been Gaudí's intention.

The public exterior, with its towers, Gothic windows, and medieval crenellations, was intended to link the building—the entire property—to the Catalan legend of Martí I the Humane. The interior, however, in its walls, ceilings, arches, and other features, recalls a muted version of another near-contemporary project, the organic surfaces inside the Casa Batlló.

The Torre Bellesguard is in many ways one of Gaudí's most original buildings, borrowing from a variety of styles, and applying those styles to a complex program of both religious and Catalanist symbolism, one that a friend said made both architect and this architecture the "most Catalan of Catalonians."

TORRE BELLESGUARD

PINNACLE OF TOWER

Courtesy of Oronoz

IT is useful and perhaps even illuminating when considering certain features of Bellesguard to remember the other projects Gaudí was developing at the same time. He had begun the Colonia Güell two years earlier, was near completion of the "educational" Nativity Façade of the Sagrada Familia and, perhaps most interestingly of all, was also starting work on the Park Güell.

While Bellesguard can be read as a compendium of medieval references—seen from its frontage it actually resembles a small Gothic lodge that has been stretched upwards—there is also something of the porter's lodge at Park Güell, barely two kilometers away, about the Bellesguard tower. It employs the three-dimensional, four-sided transverse cross first seen in the Colegio de Santa Teresa and by now a signature motif in Gaudí's work. To all intents and purposes this is a "sober," although fictionally austere, version of the cross tower at the gates of the Park that some critics have read as an elephant's trunk. Although the rusticated slate cladding has flower—again, possibly rose—patterns, the effect is a romanticized version of medievalism.

At its pinnacle, however, Gaudí kindles a blaze of light—perhaps literally intended as a beacon. The transverse cross is sheathed in dazzling red and white *trencadis*—symbolism aplenty for those who want to read it—supported by a cylinder of red stripes on yellow, the Catalan flag, which, as above, is also found below.

The interior and exterior of the Bellesguard tower are very different in style and impression. No-one could imagine that inside this Gothic temple were soft, warm colors and fantastic forms. Gaudí's struggle with austerity and embellishment is witnessed in full here. The sharp, man-made edges of the tower are in contrast and relief to the curves and bulges of the interior which reflect a more organic shape. It is almost as if he is daring one to enter and then rewarding the intrepid explorer once the first steps have been made. Perhaps this is the form which his fear of death takes; the promise of what is "on the other side" being a central tenet of Catholicism.

TORRE BELLESGUARD

INTERIOR

Courtesy of Oronoz

THE hints of Mudéjar and Arabic and the soft, almost fleshy walls also conceal something else about the Torre Bellesguard: these anachronistic features often appear because Gaudí needed to disguise utterly functional details such as air vents and light sources. This was, again, his famous attention to prosaic detail showing itself, going against the dictum of form-over-function, making the form fit the function.

Perhaps most remarkable, however, is the fact that Gaudí managed to fuse all these contradictory styles—medieval, Moorish, organic, permutations and mutations of any of the above—into a cohesive whole. Moreover, he did so while pursuing the most complex "editorial" line in any of his projects outside the Sagrada Familia and the Park Güell. While the Torre Bellesguard serves the demands placed on it by the pressure of symbolism—both Catalanist and religious—its interior is an almost womb-like private domestic space, awash with light, soothing and above all intimate. The play between interior and exterior even manages, in its dramatically exaggerated perspectives, to include a note of humor. Some of the credit for the interior must go to Gaudí's colleague Doménec Sugrañes, who completed the interior and contributed much of the tilework and features such as the dado lines. Yet the overall design remains that of Gaudí, and for one of his lesser-known private houses the Torre Bellesguard remains one of his most complex.

TORRE BELLESGUARD

INTERIOR WITH ROOF/ARCH DETAILS

Courtesy of Oronoz

INSIDE the Torre Bellesguard, Gaudí left bare the handsome brickwork in both the roof and the cellar, following his philosophy of an "honest" use of materials and forms. In the domestic spaces, however, he introduced a technique he had begun on the ceiling of the Güell Pavilions and which would come to fruition on the ceilings of the Casa Milà. Gaudí covered most of the interior walls, columns, and arches with a smooth, flowing skin of pure white plaster, softening any hard edges or corners to give the interior an almost silky texture. There is possibly significance in the fact that he was working for a woman and attempted a feminine interior, one that is in some ways as mystifying to us as it seems the feminine sex was to Gaudí.

While the tiling and dado rails are Sugrañes' design, the exquisite stained-glass features are Gaudí's own. Instead of a traditional religious image however, Gaudí had, surprisingly, intended the stained-glass work to be a tribute to Venus, the goddess of love, although it is uncertain how, if it had been completed, this would have looked. Almost inevitably this feature was the one left unfinished when he abandoned work on the house.

Given the medieval panoply of the exterior (with its reference to battlements and defenses on the outside protecting its precious interior), the Venus window might seem to strike an incongruous tone, not least in a house designed for a widow by an ascetic and probably celibate single male architect. Possibly the window was a request from his client. It is quite likely, however, that here was yet another reference to Catalan legend: in 1409, Bellesguard was the site of King Martí I the Humane's marriage to Margarida de Prades.

CASA BATLLÓ, NUMBER 43 PASSEIG DE GRACIA *1904–6*

Courtesy of Paul Rafferty / Arcaid

THE gloves came off with Gaudí's first house on the Passeig de Gracia. The sinuous animal shapes, the hints of bone and skeleton, and the unbridled use of iridescent color fused together in a synthesis of Gaudí's architectural obsessions in a way that still stupefies observers today. While the Casa Milà is usually held to be his greatest secular architectural achievement, the Casa Batlló is the project where he most let his imagination and invention run wild. It is also the house that a visitor compared to Hansel and Gretel's, provoking peals of delighted laughter from the architect.

It was designed for yet another wealthy Barcelonan cotton baron, Josep Batlló i Casanovas, who, aptly enough, wanted a *nueva casa* to compete with the other startling structures appearing in this wealthy part of Barcelona's Eixample. (It would end up in a shoving contest with the neighboring Amatller house by Josep Puig i Cadafalch and two other *modernista* buildings in a single block that became known as the "Quarter of Discord.") In fact, Batlló already occupied the building—said on its original construction thirty years earlier to have been the most boring apartment house in Barcelona. He commissioned Gaudí to reshape its simple, blockish exterior and interior. Little could the cotton baron have imagined what monstrous beauty would hatch from this dull chrysalis.

It is tempting to imagine the delight which Gaudí took in transforming this typical, dull, man-made home of an industrial baron into such a fantastical, fairy-tale setting. Little wonder that he was so pleased when someone dared to mention Hansel and Gretel. Such things had obviously been missed in the past and it must have been pleasing for Gaudí to have recognition for his child-like playfulness in creating such a wondrous building.

The contrast with the uniformity of its surroundings is fantastic—witness the house on the right (opposite). It would be a fine house in any European city (and that is the point of its design) and impossible to place directly if it were not for its fabulous neighbor. Everyone instantly recognizes Barcelona and the hand of Gaudí when shown the Casa Batlló.

CASA BATLLÓ, NUMBER 43 PASSEIG DE GRACIA

FAÇADE (DAYTIME)

Courtesy of Paul Rafferty/Arcaid

GIVEN that the Casa Batlló was a conventional rectangular building in which the same floorplan was repeated on virtually all six floors and in the attic space, Gaudí's transformation of the structure seems all the more remarkable. The bone and limb shapes that had been peeking out of other buildings here become utterly explicit, right down to the elephantine "legs" on which the building faces on the street. Here, again, Gaudí flouted city planning regulations by deliberately extending these bulky limbs two feet out on to the pavement. Here, again, he got his own way against the wishes of the city planning regulators.

The window frames retain a faint echo of art nouveau, although the jointed bone-like supports in the middle of the frames give them a humanoid form. Joan Bergós, Gaudí's long-time assistant, suggests in *Gaudí, el hombre y las obras* that they in fact resemble mouths that are unable to close because of the toothpicks jamming them open (a rather infernal image for so jocular a façade, at least in daytime). Bone shapes—suggesting septum, eyebrow or clavicle—in the horizontals between floors stress the anthropomorphic tone. This effect becomes increasingly extreme the further up the façade we travel, until we reach the startling metamorphosis on the roof, where Gaudí's mother-of-pearl stegosaurus, glimpsed in earlier buildings, awaits us in all its glory.

Before moving on to consider the Casa Batlló's most dramatic view, the illuminated night-time version, we should pause for a number of rather more prosaic considerations. Apart from a handful of religious inscriptions almost hidden among the upper reaches of the façade, Gaudí's Catalanist and religious themes have disappeared almost entirely here (although they return with a bang in the interior). It is almost as though the architect abandoned his aesthetic and cultural obsessions to essay this exercise in flamboyance as a riposte to his critics. The modern observer might also want to consider just what the occupants thought of living inside this candy fantasia, and what the cotton baron thought this dreamlike confection said about his social standing.

Casa Batlló, Number 43 Passeig de Gracia

Façade (night view)

Courtesy of Alex Bartel / Arcaid

THE Batlló façade, and Gaudí's intended effects, come into their own at night. The difference between the daytime and night-time view is so marked—the former fanciful, the latter unequivocally malevolent—that they might be two entirely different buildings. Interior and exterior lighting throws the animal balconies into stark and even scary relief. Remember, it is morning when Hansel and Gretel stumble upon the witch's house of sugar and they see it as a safe haven, a rescue from their troubles. It is only later that they realize that it's a trap, a place of horror within which they are to be eaten.

The upper balconies are clearly intended to resemble the skulls of small animals—cats, or foxes, or perhaps even bats—and the night view seems to suggest a squadron of the last flying towards the observer in formation. They can only have trouble in mind. Diverted by the drama in the balconies, it is easy for the eye to miss subtler effects in the fabric of the façade. In between the animal balconies, the surface of the building appears to ripple, like muscle and skin over vestigial bones.

In day or night lighting, the effect seems to suggest that the entire structure is a living, sentient organism capable of motion, possibly of walking, and equipped for defensive and perhaps even offensive maneuvers. Having alluded to the dragon so many times in earlier buildings, did Gaudí let it loose on the Passeig de Gracia?

If Gaudí was such a religious zealot then he clearly knew and understood the idea of how difficult it is for a rich man to enter the kingdom of heaven. One could say that the daytime view of Casa Batlló represents a certain view of heaven. One could equally imagine that the night-time view is one of the gates of Hell.

Gaudí's use of symbolism is so rich—or so easily and richly interpreted—that it is impossible to tell what his own intentions were. Especially here.

CASA BATLLÓ, NUMBER 43 PASSEIG DE GRACIA

ANIMAL BALCONY

Courtesy of Richard Bryant/Arcaid

IF the monster at Number 43 *was* contentedly digesting the textile manufacturer and his next of kin, Josep Marià Jujol gave it a complexion that suggested a sprite or other fairytale figure from Spenser's *Faerie Queene* or one of Shakespeare's occult fantasies; an Ariel, perhaps. The flesh of the Casa Batlló actually sparkles.

The *trencadis* mosaics forming the lustrous membrane over the house's skeleton were the subtlest that Jujol had yet produced, this time employing glass as well as broken tile, and colored discs which echoed the circular patterning in the glazing of the first-floor windows. The mosaics here are entirely abstract, although not for the sake of abstraction: this was simply to achieve Gaudí's desired effect of gradation and texture. And yet something else seems to be happening, particularly in the colored discs, which as well as looking forward to Julian Schnabel's 1980s crockery art also feature hazy smudges of different colors. They might be imaginary maps, or fogged representational images. This is something that would appear in more explicit form in the interior of the Casa Milà, where the interior color scheme in fact borrows some of the effects (if not the intentions) of Monet and the French Impressionists.

There is also religious imagery here, although so attenuated as to be almost subliminal. As well as the semi-concealed religious images and texts planted in the upper levels of the building, small details around the façade are resonant with symbolic meaning. The stone pelican roosting on the lowest of the three balconies to the right is about to take flight for the Sagrada Familia, where it will appear in the tree of life tableau as a symbol of both the holy ghost and the resurrection.

Casa Batlló, Number 43 Passeig de Gracia

Roof and tower

Courtesy of Richard Bryant/Arcaid

IF the roof is the lair of the stegosaurus, one of the most remarkable things about it is that some of the most dramatic features are actually hidden from view, again suggesting that Gaudí intended some of his effects as entirely private visual conceits or puns. The huge ribbed humpback is clad on one side by armor plating resembling an armadillo's (Gaudí intended the green tiling to resemble a heaving sea), while on the other side it is covered with *trencadis* fragments producing a subtle white-into-orange sheen. The spine is dotted with bulbous green and blue vertebrae, suggesting that these might be organisms themselves, while the flowing lines where roof meets façade are edged with other armatures of saurian bone and joint.

As with the designs for the Casa Calvet and other domestic projects, the topmost balcony is in fact a decorative detail to camouflage an access window for a pair of winches visible at either side. These would have been used to haul furniture up to the windows of the apartments below.

It appears that Gaudí, in his improvisational way with building plans, decided to add one of his trademark religious references only on the most inaccessible (and virtually invisible: it can only really be seen with binoculars) point of the façade. The tower to the left of the roof, ending in what might be a clump of garlic, is topped by his signature four-pointed transverse cross, and anagrams referring to the holy family are inscribed on the tower itself. The intent behind this is unclear. While such messages were commonplace on Gaudí's more sober buildings—even the Casa Milà—here they jar with the hallucinatory excesses of the design. It is possible that Gaudí, while indulging this phantasmagorical construction, also wanted to point out that religion can embrace humor, fantasy, and the absurd. Equally it could be his message to God that he was working in His name and not just for the money man in order to glorify the creation of wealth for the sake of wealth.

CASA BATLLÓ

CASA BATLLÓ,
NUMBER 43 PASSEIG DE GRACIA

CHIMNEYS

Courtesy of AISA

GAUDÍ continued his curious camouflage action with the Casa Batlló chimneys and air vents, the latter made necessary because this fairytale structure boasted central heating, almost unheard of in Barcelona at the time, and other state-of-the-art domestic services. Yet, again, these are also obscured from view, almost entirely tucked behind the stegosaurus's back. There are two nests, or families, of chimneys/vents on the roof, variations on Gaudí's *espantabrujeras* from El Capricho and elsewhere. Their square columns feature jigsaw abstracts of *trencadis* mosaic, the heads of the witch-scarers bearing either sunburst or mask-like patterns. The members of both *espantabrujera* platoons are each topped by a spherical *trencadis* approximation of what might be a Christmas tree bauble. Joan Bergós, however, detected something quite fascinating in one of the two sets of chimneys. Rather than rising vertically, these depart the roof at a 45-degree angle before turning vertical. In another fascinating twist in the engineer Gaudí's mind, Bergós says that the rising square columns have in them the helical spin of the columns seen in buildings such as the Colegio de Santa Teresa. There, flat, square tiles were laid on top of each other in such a way that the square column would appear to twist into a cylindrical spiral as it rose upwards. These *espantabrujeras*, says Bergós, have the same helical spin that has been observed in fires and whirlwinds, suggesting more allusions to alchemy, weather, and nature reified into brick and tile.

CASA BATLLÓ,
NUMBER 43 PASSEIG DE GRACIA

INTERIOR

Courtesy of AISA

GAUDÍ also took the stegosaurus indoors at Number 43. Its knobbly spine is the line the staircase takes up into the first-floor apartment of the Batlló family, and its bones bulge from interior walls. As with the interior walls of the Torre Bellesguard, these were smoothed into skin or dune formations using plaster and paint, here giving the effect of being inside a living organism. Like the endoscopy images seemingly echoed in the corridors of the Colegio de Santa Teresa, the rippling organic bulges really do seem to suggest that this is an architecture of peristalsis, digestion.

Many of the interior decorative features—doors, frames, peepholes, moldings, screens, and other details—are a variation on Gaudí's increasingly mutant take on art nouveau, although there are hints of vegetable forms appearing here too.

It would appear that here Gaudí has abandoned many of the cultural themes that run through his work. Yet at one point at the center of the house, Catalanism re-emerges with some force. A fireplace on the first floor could be a nouveau mushroom shape or a mouth from the steps of the Park Güell. Its presence, however—in a house equipped with state-of-the-art central heating—suggests that Gaudí is alluding to the *llar de foc*, the hearth that sat at the heart of the Catalan family home, or *casa pairal*, itself a core symbol of Catalan culture. In *Barcelona*, Robert Hughes explains that the *casa pairal* was more central to the Catalan sense of self than the Englishman's castle-home. The *llar de foc* was an inglenook in which every member of the family, from the father down to the lowliest servant, had and knew their place. For it to rematerialize here, in Gaudí's penultimate domestic building, suggests a certain symbolism at play.

Casa Milà (La Pedrera) *1906–12*

Courtesy of Colin Dixon / Arcaid

JUST as quickly as he had ignited a firework display on the Passeig de Gracia, Gaudí swiftly doused it. His next project, at Number 92, would be almost snowy white, and devoted to the Virgin Mary. Some have wondered why, having just produced the Batlló house, and with the Sagrada Familia demanding more and more of his time, Gaudí should have accepted another commission. It is quite likely that he was intrigued by the size of the project—this was in fact two houses, straddling a street corner at a major intersection. As such, it would be his largest secular work. It is also possible that he was unable to resist the opportunity to design another building dedicated to the cult of the Virgin Mary. It is equally possible that after the bravura display of the Casa Batlló, Gaudí felt a desire to cap off his secular work with something serene, spiritual, and graceful.

The Casa Milà, which from its stone-like appearance was swiftly nicknamed "La Pedrera," the quarry, by the media and coffee-house wags, was built for businessman Pere Milà Camps and his wife Rosario Segimon Artells. However, Gaudí's original commission had come from the previous owner of one of the two houses incorporated into the plot.

It is the Gaudí house where we should most take note of the roof and skyline, not least because, once again, the architect deliberately overshot the height limitations imposed on the area, as well as pushing his building out into the street as he had done with Number 43. When the Casa Milà was built, Barcelona was a distinctly low-rise city. La Pedrera was the biggest building in the area, with clear sightlines to the Sagrada Familia. Today, unfortunately, its effect is dwarfed by the growth of the city.

Casa Milà (La Pedrera)

Corner façade

Courtesy of Colin Dixon/Arcaid

THE position and shape of the Casa Milà are both unusual. When the city planner Ildefons Cerdá laid out the Eixample, he included many public parks and had the corners of the intersections chamfered—that is, the apex was sliced off diagonally, making each block an irregular octagon. This created space and light at the intersections and, unintentionally, improved cornering vision for drivers when cars appeared on Barcelona's streets. The Casa Milà sits on one such chamfer, and is wrapped around three frontages, a shape that lends itself to the creation of a large courtyard or air well at its center.

Gaudí took his work with prefabrication even further here, coming up with what might almost be a *fin-de-siècle* equivalent to the modern technique of curtain wall construction. There are no load-bearing walls in La Pedrera: the façade, floors, and interior walls sit on a slender skeleton of girders, which enabled Gaudí or the inhabitants to alter interior spaces at will. Gaudí even commented that the flexibility within the structure might make it suitable for conversion into a grand hotel some day. (It is now a gallery, office, and museum space, administered by an artistic foundation financed by a bank.)

Casa Milà (La Pedrera)

Side elevation

Courtesy of Colin Dixon / Arcaid

ALTHOUGH it doesn't look it, La Pedrera is another building that Gaudí left unfinished, possibly because of a disagreement with the owners over a disputed bill. He had intended to top the building with a large (but not outsize) group of sculptures representing the Virgin and the holy family. Popular myth blew this up into mountainous proportions, and further claimed that, in the manner of an iceberg, there was more of the house underground than over (it has a modest basement, with an ingenious area to house service pipes and vents, but no more).

Although the Park Güell elephant may have modeled for the columns that protrude into the street, the animal shapes of the Batlló here recede into an approximation of rock (in fact limestone and Portland cement). The appearance is pure artifice—more cladding, in fact—but people have read anything from honeycombs to African cliff dwellings to seascapes into its façade. While it was being built, Barcelona's newspapers published cartoons suggesting it was going to be a garage for zeppelins, or a vivarium for giant snails. French prime minister Georges Clemenceau is alleged to have returned from a trip to the city marveling that in Barcelona "they build houses for dragons!"

Gaudí doesn't appear to have divulged the actual inspiration to any of the colleagues who subsequently wrote about or commented on his work. The most likely influence is the regional landscape, either at the Fra Guerau gorge near Tarragona, the cliffs at Pareis in northern Mallorca, or the cliffs and quarries of Garraf. Given the absence of any overt Catalanist features, it is possible that Gaudí thought his notional "stone" Marian monument would be a tribute to the very earth of Catalonia, one that would be both literally and figuratively sublime.

CASA MILÀ (LA PEDRERA)

BALCONIES

Courtesy of Richard Bryant / Arcaid

IT is the balconies that elicit suggestions of cliff, wave or beehive, even though they are in fact surprisingly uniform—in fact, taken in its entire length, the façade has a highly programmatic and virtually symmetrical plan. The sinuous undulations of the façade are a good place to stop and consider Gaudí's position in his time.

La Pedrera was contemporary with Domènech i Montaner's extravagant Palau de la Música Catalana and other major *modernista* projects. During La Pedrera's construction its younger sibling, Casa Batlló, was slugging it out with another Domènech i Montaner building and one by Josep Puig i Cadafalch for dominance of the "Block of Discord" just down the street. Gaudí has often been lumped in with these high-art *modernistas*, but La Pedrera's flowing rock fields bear no relation whatsoever to the demented crenellations and flourishes of *modernisme*.

Where the *modernistas* were concerned with style over function—Domènech's Palau de la Música is an acoustical disaster, with street noise audible in the auditorium—Gaudí saw all aspects of a building as an organic whole. And apart from certain troglodytic dwellings in parts of Mediterranean Europe, there is no other architecture in the whole of Europe that resembles La Pedrera.

In some ways it is unfair to compare Gaudí with his contemporaries since his work is clearly not of this world. As these balconies suggest he could work under water, in the air (he did, after all, build higher than any other architect of his time), and in waves which were, on the surface, hard to calculate.

This is architecture that has burnt its passport, gone native, feral even. In fact, this is—as Gaudí had hinted at elsewhere—architecture that is slowly dissolving, and he left two clues to this in the balconies.

CASA MILÀ (LA PEDRERA)

BALCONY FEATURES

Courtesy of Colin Dixon/Arcaid

THE monumental sculpture intended for the roof was by no means the only detail abandoned when Gaudí stopped work on the Casa Milà. Small features of the interior, including painting and furniture details, were left unfinished. Perhaps the most intriguing job left undone, however, was the finishing touch on the balconies. While La Pedrera has been read as a monument to stone, and by extension the Catalan landscape, Gaudí in fact intended it to be covered by plant growth. He included complex windowboxes for the balconies in his plans, and even envisaged an automatic watering system feeding the plant life. If his plans had been realized, the Casa Milà would have been a living rustic landscape in the heart of the city.

Beneath the greenery, the structure itself would appear to be dissolving by erosion, both by wind and rain—Gaudí actually took into account the atmospheric effects on his buildings, and even the likely effect of parasites such as fungi and microbes. While the stone itself would not literally weather noticeably—although pollution would blacken the façade within a few generations—he helped the effect along in a way that had first appeared on the Casa Batlló and would be writ large across the Sagrada Familia. His designs for the metalwork on the Milà balconies, executed by other craftsmen, figure plant life at various stages of decay. This dissolving effect would later cascade down the exterior walls of the Sagrada Familia.

CASA MILÀ (LA PEDRERA)

ROOFSCAPE

Courtesy of Richard Bryant / Arcaid

THE attic space of the Casa Milà contains another surprise, a honeycomb of catenary arches that echo through the space with a rhythm that is almost hypnotic. These signature forms from earlier Gaudí buildings were installed to support the rooftop sculpture that never materialized. As the façade and attic roofs flow along the top of the building, so the roof itself rises and falls in rhythm with the attic spaces, although in stepped and tiled progression. Roof access from the attic, chimneys, and air vents dressed the roofscape, although it is a far less dramatic landscape than those atop the Palau and Park Güell or the Casa Batlló rooftops. It is likely that the roof was left more or less clear for the Marian sculpture and only decorated when that too was abandoned.

Rumor about the proportions of the proposed statue also fostered another urban myth about the Casa Milà, that the statue was not finished (a scale maquette had been made) because the owners feared that it might invite retribution by anticlerical groups in the city. This followed the Setmana Tragica workers' uprising of 1909, which was extremely hostile towards the Church. Gaudí expert Joan Bassegoda i Nonell, now retired as the professor of the Catedra Gaudí study center in Barcelona, points out in his *La Pedrera de Gaudí* that the reason the statue never appeared was Senõr Milà's low opinion of the maquette. Polite negotiations were continuing over the statue as late as 1911, two years after the Setmana Tragica, but finally Milà got his own way and the idea for the statue was quietly dropped.

Casa Milà (La Pedrera)

Roof and chimneys

Courtesy of Richard Bryant / Arcaid

ALTHOUGH they lack the dazzling color work of either the Palau Güell or the Casa Batlló, Gaudí's chimneys and air vents for the La Pedrera roof are his most dramatic ever. In fact, these were the chimneys that inspired the popular nickname of *espantabrujeras*, the witch-scarers seen elsewhere on Gaudí's buildings, but nowhere as visible as here.

More than either the Palacio Güell or El Capricho chimneys, these are of an unmistakably militaristic mien—they even seem to prefigure the imposing head sculptures of Naum Gabo. Only a handful boast *trencadis* tiling, and that is almost monochrome, or employs polychrome tiles to effect a gray-white sheen. Some are undressed stone or concrete, others use found materials—rubble, and in one case fragments of champagne bottles, said to be the remnants of a celebration on the site—in a fashion that seems to sniff Dada in the air.

The chimneys are also noticeably varied, some suggesting warrior-like armored bodies below the heads, others in identical groups that seem to invite reading as members of the cast in a drama being enacted on the roof. (A claim that the entire tableau represents the flight from Egypt has been dismissed by Gaudí scholars, who point out that the tableau was only completed after Gaudí abandoned work on the building.) Again, some of the groups are twining in the helical spin that Bergós spied on the Batlló roof. If Gaudí intended them to be read as allegory, he left no clues. It is just as likely that the architect who peppered his work with talaiots, fraudulent rock landscapes, and *espantabrujeras* intended them to echo the bucolic landscape represented in the façade.

CASA MILÀ (LA PEDRERA)

COURTYARD

Courtesy of Richard Bryant / Arcaid

GAUDÍ extended the air of decay into the metalwork and other details he designed for the Milà courtyard. Here, perhaps as befits such a controversial yet popular building, the Casa Milà inspired at least one other urban myth, this time about its interior. A taxi driver is thought to have told a customer that Gaudí was building an apartment block where people could drive right up to their front doors; he himself had driven a fare there. In the manner of Chinese whispers, La Pedrera was declared the world's first drive-in apartment building, with predictable consequences among the city's humorists and cartoonists. (*Vanity Fair* satirical artist Bruce McCall was still milking a similar joke set in Manhattan in the 1980s.) While not strictly true—although Gaudí had toyed with but rejected the idea as impractical—the myth does point up something that is often lost in the fog of medievalism that clings to Gaudí's work: behind that cladding, he was a thoroughly modern architect and housing engineer.

As with the Palau Güell, the Casa Milà did indeed have a courtyard that people could drive either carriages or cars into. In fact, it overlapped with the era of the car to the extent that a Rolls-Royce owner living in the Casa Milà persuaded Gaudí to widen the courtyard for him to swing his Rolls into the parking space. This, however, was as far as any horse-drawn or motorized vehicle could go. Residents and visitors ascended either by a beautiful glass-covered staircase or an interior staircase to electric lifts which were the only means of accessing the upper floors. (A separate flight of stairs served domestic staff and tradesmen.) Gaudí continued the molding of the façade up the interior of the courtyard, even placing witch-scarers on air and steam vents inside it, and sloped its upper walls outwards to allow light to fall into the courtyard.

Casa Milà (La Pedrera)

Courtyard designs

Courtesy of Colin Dixon/Arcaid

IF the only color on the exterior of La Pedrera was to be the windowbox gardens and a blush of *trencadis* tiles on the roof, Gaudí returned to his idea of painted stone in the upper levels of the courtyard. The color scheme was executed by a team of artists including Ivo Pascual, who had worked with Gaudí on the restoration of the Palma de Mallorca cathedral. It was designed to trap and enhance the sunlight falling into the air well (just as the shell-like glass entrance canopy strung across it was to deflect Barcelona's winter rains). Yet again, this would appear to be a semi-private whim of Gaudí's; although the inhabitants might appreciate what they could glimpse of the lower details in the courtyard paintwork, much of it would only be seen from the upper storeys, through small windows in service areas inhabited for the most part by servants. This too seems to be part of Gaudí's obsession with perfection for even the most minor detail of a building.

Perhaps hoping to beautify such a prosaic space, the interior harks back to both the shapes and colors of the Casa Batlló, although in a far more restrained fashion. The rockface has hints of bone or sand dune (something that would recur in the interior), and the color work shifts from strong purples and blues to soft pinks and oranges. Higher up among the windows of the courtyard, these colors and the techniques used to apply them would begin to resemble Impressionism. It is almost as though Gaudí and his painters wanted to include a secret homage to Monet and his garden at Giverny—Monet's monumental *Water Lilies* canvas was completed the year Gaudí began building La Pedrera. This effect would also flow inside the building, where if anything it is intensified.

Casa Milà (La Pedrera)

Ceiling designs

Courtesy of AISA

ALTHOUGH it is the most accessible of Gaudí's buildings, the interior of La Pedrera has, over the years, been the most compromised of all his designs. Flats were installed in the attic spaces, and shops squared out the semi-basement areas around the frontage. Tenants made unsympathetic alterations, although the worst offender was probably Doña Rosario herself, who actually had some of Gaudí's interior features secretly covered up after his death.

The building, interior and exterior, reached its nadir around the beginning of the 1980s, when it was blackened by pollution and appeared abandoned. While some details are lost forever, painstaking restoration has returned some aspects of La Pedrera to near-pristine condition—none more so than the surfaces in the interior.

As on the exterior, this is no longer a journey through the digestive tract of some mythic beast, in the Casa Batlló manner. Like the interiors of the Güell Pavilions and the Torre Bellesguard, these display delicately crafted plaster moldings intended to subvert the rigid planes of conventional interiors. Gaudí insisted that pure planes did not exist in nature or indeed in architecture itself—flat surfaces are inevitably bowed and pitted by age and wear. These effects reach their most expressive point in the ceiling moldings, where waves and ridges, highlighted by either daylight or electrical lighting, suggest miniature drifting desert landscapes, or the improbable whorls of confectionery such as meringues. Here too, however, are hints of the "dissolving" architecture on the exterior; delicate paper-like layers seem to be detaching from the ceiling in places, decaying and fading away. Again, this is artifice, but between here and the façades of the Sagrada Familia, one begins to wonder if Gaudí isn't saying something about the transitory, ephemeral nature of existence.

CASA MILÀ (LA PEDRERA)

INTERIOR COLUMNS

Courtesy of AISA

IF La Pedrera is the most democratic of all of Gaudí's buildings (the lack of public access to most of his buildings remains a mystery, given his status), it also allows the visitor to see that even sympathetic renovation hasn't entirely restored all his intended features for the interior. While the upper-level *piso*, or apartment, has been restored and furnished in the style of the era, including a number of pieces of Gaudí furniture, spaces lower in the building have been drastically altered from the original. Redistribution of space has resulted in some columns being stranded in rather weird positions, and others have been unsympathetically absorbed into alterations in the structure.

Yet the interior pillars of the Casa Milà also include some of his most striking work here. From comments to colleagues, Gaudí appears to have been thinking of vegetable images and the idea of a decaying natural world when he designed these: some of them flow into undulating, polychromatic ceilings, suggesting the undersides of vegetable growth. Some are un-dressed and pitted stone, but inscribed with designs and fragments of the devotional Marian text that Gaudí had hoped would flow around the entire building.

Others fuse with contoured features in the ceiling, notably in the recesses of the courtyard, suggesting stalk-like growths. The message could be that we are all supported by our organic structure, yet it fades and dies, taking our physical form with us. We all grow toward the light, in this case that of Mary, mother of God.

Given the plan to dedicate much of the project to Mary, the references to landscape on the interior and the organic allusions on both exterior and interior, it seems that Gaudí intended something like a subliminal Christian–pantheist program to the completed building.

GAUDÍ BED *1908*

Courtesy of AISA

LIKE his chairs, benches and other designs for domestic furniture, Gaudí's bed—not actually his own, but one designed for a client, and now on display at the Gaudí Museum in the Park Güell—was far more reserved than the daring experiments in shape and line seen in his buildings. Where his buildings, or at least their exteriors, resembled the product of a limitless imagination, with his furniture the function very much drove the form. His furniture had a job to do—accommodate whoever was using it—and this had to take precedence over Gaudí's desire to incorporate religious or Catalanist themes in his designs.

We can see, however, certain Gaudí themes in his bed, not least the Gothic bulkiness and the allusions to medieval crenellations in both the foot and the head of the bed. The comforting solidity of his bed, like the sturdiness of his day furniture, probably also feeds into the rusticity, real or stylized, that is never too far away in his work. It is, however, rather different from the actual bed that Gaudí slept in during the last decades of his life. When he abandoned the house in the Park Güell and moved into his studio at the Sagrada Familia in order to devote himself to his life-work, Gaudí slept the few hours that he did sleep in a rickety metal four-poster that seemed in constant danger of collapsing on its sleeping inhabitant.

EL TEMPLO EXPIATORIO
DE LA SAGRADA FAMILIA *1883–1926*

Courtesy of John Edward Linden/Arcaid

IT is a measure of Gaudí's status, and perhaps the power of his wealthy friends, that he was asked to take over work on the Sagrada Familia in 1883, at the age of 31. He had not built a single house at the time—the Casa Vicens only began construction that year—and yet he was offered the job without even having to bid for it.

The church had been under construction since 1881, when its original architect, Francisco Villar, was commissioned by the Spiritual Association for Devotion to Saint Joseph (patriarch of the Holy Family) to build a new, expiatory church. After the waves of anticlerical violence that followed the Carlist wars, the Spanish Roman Catholic establishment wanted to restore the Church to its position of influence in society. Simultaneously, it wanted to make a stand against the increasing secularisation that attended Spain's transition into an industrial society. The "expiatory" church, atoning for the sins of modern society, would be a counterweight to the swing towards atheism—not to mention its corollary, socialism. It would also be a beacon for the revival in spirituality that the Church was seeking to promote.

It seems that Villar soon ran into trouble with the Association and resigned the commission. At the suggestion of Barcelonan architect Joan Martorell, Gaudí, who was already moving in influential religious and political circles in the city, was offered the job. So on 3 November 1883 he took charge of the project that would both make him globally famous and yet frustrate his ambitions to see it completed in his lifetime.

It would have been an irony that was not lost on the architect that the greatest project of his life had been commissioned in order to restore the place of Catholicism in society. So much of Gaudí's work seemed to have struggled with the idea that the ancient is always with us and that it has to meld perfectly with the modern in order to be relevant. So much of his work seemed designed to bring the glory of God to people, however obtusely (so much was hidden within the buildings). At his death Gaudí was living among the unfinished debris of the Sagrada Familia, a poor and forgotten man.

EL TEMPLO EXPIATORIO DE LA SAGRADA FAMILIA
SAGRADA FAMILIA AND NATIVITY FAÇADE

Courtesy of AISA

HAVING inherited the ground plan laid out by Villar, including the completed crypt, Gaudí altered the plan to suit his preferences. As he designed it, it bears a similarity to the layout of the Dom cathedral in Cologne, which, while unapologetically Gothic, met with Gaudí's approval. His plan was for a basilica, the classic rectangular church shape, with five naves running its length and three lateral naves forming a traditional Latin cross around the altar. Above the point where these three met would be a great ceiling supported by the most ambitious columns Gaudí ever designed.

Several other chapels would also be incorporated into the space. It is perhaps another measure of Gaudí's ambition that his church or temple was almost as big as Barcelona's cathedral and its towering façades as high as those of Cologne. (As Gaudí's piety became more and more pronounced, the project was nicknamed the "cathedral of the poor," and even though it lacks a cathedra—the bishop's seat—or see—the bishop's nominal authority—Gaudí himself was heard to refer to it as a "cathedral.")

Gaudí's style has been called "proto-modernist" or "neo-Gothic," and in his last, greatest work, all the styles he essayed throughout his career can be found. As well as a rich and complex symbolic scheme, the temple would employ virtually all of the techniques and styles he had developed in other buildings, as well as a number of other innovations or improvements devised solely for the Sagrada Familia. As in other projects, his own idiosyncratic readings of Gothic styles would be fused with organic forms and his conviction that color was not only essential to architecture but that it had a religious symbolism as well.

EL TEMPLO EXPIATORIO DE LA SAGRADA FAMILIA

PASSION FAÇADE

Courtesy of AISA

THE temple's three main façades—the Nativity, Passion and Glory façades—would each feature four towers, constituting a total of twelve towers representing the apostles. They would also echo the roles of the apostles as Christ's bishops on Earth with their allusions to the bishop's crozier, mitre and ring. Despite its appearance of eldritch medievalism, the temple in fact employed Gaudí's innovative construction technologies alongside traditional forms. Much of the superstructure is built of prefabricated materials, as are many of the ornamental details on the exterior.

Gaudí's guiding vision was a church—and, inside it, a religion—that would bring its congregation as close as possible to the living experience of their belief. In pursuit of this, he stripped the temple of much of the excess of Gothic adornment, and cleared the interior space to give the congregation the greatest visual and ritual access to the mass. As he had done at the Colonia crypt—his attempted "dry run" at the Sagrada Familia—he turned to the tree and the arch to find new ways of supporting such a monumental structure.

As a private project overseen by a private organisation, the Association, the new temple was funded entirely by donation, a factor that contributed to sizeable delays in its construction. Shifts in Barcelonan, and global, politics and economics would also affect its progress. Yet early in the project Gaudí commented that "cathedrals" were intended to be the work of different architects over generations and perhaps even longer. The Sagrada Familia's northerly counterpart, Cologne's Dom, took the best part of 500 years to complete.

El Templo Expiatorio de la Sagrada Familia

NATIVITY TOWERS

Courtesy of AISA

THE four towers of the Nativity façade—including that of St Barnabas, the only tower Gaudí saw completed—have themselves become a sign, or ideogram, and not just for the Sagrada, Gaudí, or Barcelona, but for Spain itself. The Nativity façade regularly "represents" Spain (perhaps to the chagrin of latter-day Catalanists) in encyclopedias and dictionaries of world-class architecture. Cartoon-like representations of the towers found their way into the signage of the 1992 Olympics in Barcelona, and decorate untold tourist souvenirs. (It is now possible in Barcelona's tourist bazaars to purchase a—probably counterfeit—T-shirt depicting Homer Simpson visiting the Sagrada Familia.) While Gaudí was forced at points to beg from door to door, even in the street, for funds to continue his church, the billions of pesetas the Gaudí "industry" now generates would probably have paid the cost to construct it while Gaudí was alive several times over.

The Nativity façade is, at least in its present configuration, the "rear" of the design. As the most recognisable, and representative, image of the temple, it at once declares Gaudí's dissatisfaction with past forms, not least in the vegetable shapes of the spires and the almost pagan decorations on their pinnacles. Critics have seen bishop's staffs, cigars, and loaves in their shapes. They also resemble, consciously or otherwise, the ribbed wooden spires of the Dom, but here made flesh and given breath. In fact, on closer observation they conceal two minor Gaudían feats of technology. But first, that stunning feast of detail beneath them.

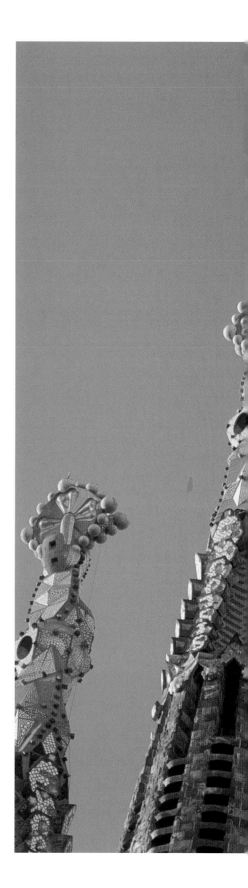

El Templo Expiatorio de la Sagrada Familia

FAÇADE OF THE NATIVITY

Courtesy of AISA

ANYONE who stands in the viewing area set back from the Nativity façade and attempts to read or memorize the detail soon realizes that the task is hopeless and abandons it. Gaudí crammed the Nativity façade—which faces east to greet the rising sun—with so much other detail around the nativity itself that the symbolism almost overloads. As well as the nativity, there are representations of the Magi and the star, the Annunciation, the child Jesus speaking in the temple, the Flight into Egypt and the Massacre of the Innocents. The last features a sword-wielding Herod modeled on-site by a workman with six toes whose extra digit Gaudí included in the sculpture in the belief that nature's quirks should also be represented here.

As with the color program of the Park Güell, Gaudí intended specific symbolism in the three doors below the façade. The door to the left signifies Hope, the central Charity, and the most rightward Faith, and Gaudí originally intended these to be colored green, blue and yellow, with representational scenes painted in the archivolts that curve over the doors. Distributed above these are figures and symbols replete with further religious meaning: the Paraclete, the initials of the Holy Trinity, Joseph piloting a ship (the Church) to safety, angelic heralds, the Catalanist holy shrine of Montserrat, and others besides. Joan Bergós reads a representation of the dual personalities of Christ—as a member of the Holy Trinity, as well as the son of Joseph and Mary—in this complex display. Gaudí seems to be pulling out all the stops in this façade—several critics have complained that it is heavy-handed, even bombastic. Stranger things are happening elsewhere here.

EL TEMPLO EXPIATORIO DE LA SAGRADA FAMILIA

NATIVITY WITH BIRDS

Courtesy of AISA

AS if to stress the inclusivity of this new, shall we say "proactive," form of Roman Catholicism, Gaudí designed the Nativity façade as a landlocked ark, including most if not all of the creatures on God's Earth. (The scorpion, whose sting ended up adorning the wall of the Finca Miralles, is excluded, as the baby scorpion Gaudí tried to study stung him when he tried to pick it up.)

Chiefly, Gaudí concentrated on birds, of land and water, the former to the right and the latter to the left of the façade. As with the flora also featured here, he intended the façade to display a range of fauna that would have been present both in the Holy Land at the time of Christ and in twentieth-century Spain. Most prominent is the pelican, but not even the lowly turkey is omitted.

Some familiar lizards and mammals, including the snake and the salamander, also appear, and there is a touch of probably unintentional ecumenism in the Buddhist turtles and tortoises supporting some of the columns. Also distributed among these images are hard-to-discern and oddly placed, distinctly secular zodiacal symbols, as seen in the Park Güell.

Most curious, however, is the effect that seems to start above the Nativity scene, in what some see as a Christmas ice cave and others as penitential tears. As we observed in the Casa Milà façade, these appear to be in the process of melting, dissolving, in what seems to be another allusion to the impermanence of the physical, the inevitable death of the flesh. Equally they could represent the tears of God on seeing how His finest creation, Man, has fared since giving His Son to them.

EL TEMPLO EXPIATORIO DE LA SAGRADA FAMILIA

THE TREE OF LIFE

Courtesy of AISA

GAUDÍ had better news to impart higher up, between the two tallest towers where a fragile bridge leaps the gap and affords some of the most astounding views of and around the temple. Although it is overshadowed, literally as well as figuratively, by the pinnacles of the towers, the vividly colored cypress, topped by a blood-red tau, the first letter in the Greek word for God, puts Gaudí's devotion to color at the center of the Nativity façade.

The tree itself is symbolic of, among other things, eternity, endurance and moral purity. The pelican at its base, lacerating its own chest to feed its young, symbolizes both the host and the resurrection. Difficult to see except in photographic reproductions, the pelican actually sits above a dazzling gold egg inscribed in bright red with the initials of Jesus Christ and assumed to be a reference to the origins of the universe and of man (as well as being another attempt by Gaudí at negating Darwin's Theory of Evolution).

The seven steps on either side of the trunk of the cypress symbolize the effort needed to attain paradise, while the white doves, fashioned in alabaster, roosting at various levels in the tree are purified souls ascending to heaven (the one at the top having presumably arrived). The almost luminous alabaster ensures that the doves are easily visible from ground level, but what is remarkable about this feature of the façade is the wealth of detail—the cross wrapped around the tau, the almost cubist planes in the tau, and the rich *trencadis* mosaics covering both features.

Again, this would seem to be Gaudí having another private word with his God.

El Templo Expiatorio de la Sagrada Familia

TOWER PINNACLES

Courtesy of AISA

GAUDÍ had been leaving sacred graffiti on his buildings for decades before he came to complete the few vertical features of the Sagrada Familia finished during his lifetime. As if the symbolic content of the Nativity façade were too brief a message in itself, the towers are pressed into service as billboards as they soar up towards, as it were, the management. Yet here again the brilliant inscriptions of "Hosannah" and "Sanctus" would be almost impossible to see from the ground, and this was at a time when few, if any, visitors were allowed to explore the towers as paying tourists are today. Once more, these seem to be semi-private details, further evidence of a private dialogue between architect and deity taking place across the fabric of the temple.

There are some fascinating smaller details that are visible in conventional views of the towers. As mentioned earlier, the Sagrada Familia features one final and minutely sublime finesse on the *trencadis* mosaics that reached maturity in the Park Güell. Towards the upper reaches of the towers, Gaudí fashioned crowns or bosses of *trencadis* that recall some of the globular shapes on the roof of the Palau Güell. Some of these rose-like shapes, and some of the stonework around them, are concave, and coated in glazed yellow or gold fragments of tile. Even up close, seen from the balconies or windows of nearby towers, these seem to radiate light, as though illuminated from within, and on a sunny day the observer has to do a double-take to see if these things aren't powered by electricity. This clever but simple device, similar to and perhaps even borrowed from the concavities sometimes found in glass Christmas decorations, would have turned the Sagrada Familia into a heavenly glitter-ball if Gaudí's plans for completion and lighting had been realized.

EL TEMPLO EXPIATORIO DE LA SAGRADA FAMILIA

TOWER INTERIORS

Courtesy of AISA

THE spires had more surprises concealed in them, not least the exquisitely designed spiral staircases that revolve, helix-like, contrariwise on either side of the façade. Modern observers will find themselves recalling the organic shapes of the Colegio de Santa Teresa arches, although for Gaudí this was probably a reference to the nautilus shell and the Golden Mean found throughout nature. Gaudí calculated the dimensions of the staircases so that the tight inner edge of the spiral would provide a welcome hand-rail without the need of a bannister.

The "eye" of the spiral was also designed with a specific purpose in mind, one that is hinted at by the downward-facing vents let out of the towers. Gaudí's concern for detail, here as elsewhere, led him to detailed research into electrical power for the building, the several options for church bell systems (plain, tuned or tubular), and the acoustics that would broadcast the sounds the bells made. As well as marking the hours, announcing mass and other services, and accompanying special ceremonies in the temple, the bells were also meant to be heard at a distance. Gaudí envisaged them accompanying processions and social events in the surrounding neighborhood—hence the downward vents, intended to broadcast the sound outwards as well as in. After investigating various alternatives, Gaudí came up with a multiple carillon of tuned bells which, when struck in various permutations, would produce sustained, organ-like chords that would reverberate through and beyond the church. The delicate whorl of the tower spirals was designed to house specially-designed tubular bells that would hang free in the center of the spiral stairs (though woe betide any on the staircase when the bell was sounded).

EL TEMPLO EXPIATORIO DE LA SAGRADA FAMILIA

ENTRANCE

Courtesy of Richard Bryant/Arcaid

THE complexity of the symbolic program that Gaudí wove into the façade of the Sagrada Familia is overwhelming in its detail and the multiplicity of its allusions. The wealth of detail suggests that Gaudí may have thought it necessary to deliver his message with such force that its intent would be inescapable. Here, in this corner of the Nativity façade, the symbolism is operating on any number of levels.

Seated observing the Nativity is Mathias, St Matthew (right), the chosen replacement for the banished Judas Iscariot and, of course, author of one of the four Testaments. Above him is a complex display of symbols for the signs of the zodiac (a possible warning against believing in anything other than the teachings of the bible?). Mathias perches on a globe and liquid approximation of Gaudí's favorite supporting shape, the helix. The pinnacle to his right echoes the saurian armor of the Casa Batlló roof, while below it the stonework is dissolving into more animal heads. The pinnacle is topped by a vegetable form, half mushroom (that natural matter which is both a sustenance and a potion), half thistle, and these vegetable forms are echoed in the recessed columns.

Perhaps the most unusual symbolism, however, is the allusion to the Gothic form. Following Viollet-le-Duc's insistence that the past should not be repeated but improved, Gaudí built his twentieth-century "cathedral" using state-of-the-art concrete techniques but clad it in a manner suggesting it could have been five hundred years old. This was the instruction of the Spiritual Association for Devotion to Saint Joseph in their original brief to Francisco Villar. Gaudí's interpretation of the instruction to "bring the Church back into the lives of the people" as it was before the Carlist wars is typical of the man. He could not bear to be constrained in his work and yet would follow instruction to the letter.

EL TEMPLO EXPIATORIO DE LA SAGRADA FAMILIA

FAÇADE OF THE PASSION

Courtesy of AISA

THE statuary of the façade of the Passion was only actually begun in 1988, when the job of interpreting Gaudí's sketches was given to the sculptor Josep Maria Subirachs. Gaudí's freehand drawings had suggested a panorama of the last week of Christ's life, from Gethsemane to Golgotha, with the crucifixion, naturally, at its center. Subirachs found himself in the middle of a controversy almost as soon as he accepted the job, largely it seems because there was and remains a vociferous lobby that considers outside work on Gaudí's project to be sacrilegious.

Subirachs spent a year immersing himself in Gaudí's works and the few written documents he left behind.

Critics such as Robert Hughes have had a bone to pick with his aesthetics, but through the various friezes, from the betrayal at cockcrow to the carrying of the cross to Calvary, Subirachs provided Gaudí with an arrestingly grim Passion. The sadness of the apostles and mourners is also unmistakable. Reaching a peak with the stark crucifixion, unadorned apart from Mary and Mary Magdalene and two skulls, the tableau resembles a stone rendering of Picasso's *Guernica*. This modern-day reference of course provides critics of Subirachs with more ammunition; they want the Sagrada to be only the work of Gaudí, so obviously it should have no relation to anything which succeeded his death.

Today, more that 125 years after it was begun, the Sagrada is not much further toward its completion that it was on the day of Gaudí's death. There is little to suggest that it ever will be. Gaudí would have appreciated the irony of it all.

El Templo Expiatorio de la Sagrada Familia

Passion façade detail

Courtesy of AISA

FRIENDS had actually tried to persuade Gaudí to construct this façade first, as it faced the city center and would have been an effective shopfront for the temple, reminding passersby of the work in progress. Gaudí declined, however, claiming the representational content of his Passion would scare people, in particular possible donors, away. He wanted this entrance, and its façade, which has the full title of The Façade of Passion and Death, to make plain that death is a "bloody business," as he told a friend.

The tableau begins with Judas's betrayal of Christ with a kiss and, although unseen here, the cock-crow by which time Christ had predicted that Judas would betray him. Josep Subirachs also included a curious detail, a mysterious stone square inscribed with seemingly random numbers. Whichever way you calculate them, they add up to 33, the age of Christ when he died. (Some have read more arcane numerology at work here.) The tableau proceeds from betrayal to execution and mourning. Although it was only begun decades after Gaudí's death, the sculptor Subirachs working from sketches left by Gaudí, it is clear that the grimness that Gaudí feared would disturb possible donors was entirely his intention, a round-the-clock hellfire sermon for the sinners of Barcelona. Little wonder, perhaps, that in 1936 some of them tried to set fire to it.

EL TEMPLO EXPIATORIO DE LA SAGRADA FAMILIA

TABLEAUX AND FRIEZES

Courtesy of Richard Bryant / Arcaid

AS well as the encyclopedic religious themes traced out across the skin of the building, Gaudí also included other, secular, images in the structure, some of them contemporary and even controversial. In the Temptation tableau, just inside the door below the Nativity façade (right), the Faith door, there are four friezes of fallible souls resisting temptation. Most of these are conventional fables of greed and avarice and the heroic struggle of the good to resist temptation. The last, however, is quite remarkable, and might almost be Gaudí trying his hand at news journalism. It figures a tormented soul being tempted by a monstrous sea-creature proffering an Orsini bomb—the classic anarchist's spherical black bomb, although here it is studded with detonators. This can only be a reference to the successive waves of insurrectionary violence that swept across Andalucia, and Barcelona, in the nineteenth century.

This would appear to be the only overtly political reference in the imagery of the Sagrada Familia. Chiefly, like the aviary of different bird species decaying on the Nativity façade, these images tended to be animal. Here too, however, Josep Carandell has detected a pervasive moral tone. There may be an unintentional polysemy—multiple meaning—at work with the turtles and tortoises that support the columns of the Nativity façade. One cannot help but note a perhaps unintentional echo of the Buddhist tortoise supporting the world, for both the land and sea breeds of these reptiles have been used to symbolize continuity and stability in both East and West. The chameleons that seem also to be dissolving represent, on the other hand, the perpetual nature of change. Carandell also sees a hierarchy among these animals. Like the banished scorpion, they appear to be positioned about the building in relation to their symbolic good or evil. Here, Gaudí's trademark snake seems to have undergone a sea-change: along with frogs, lizards, salamanders and other faintly demonic creatures, the snake seems to have reverted to its Edenic role, and is among the animals excluded from the temple.

EL TEMPLO EXPIATORIO DE LA SAGRADA FAMILIA

TOWER INSCRIPTIONS

Courtesy of Richard Bryant/Arcaid

AT the very heights of the Sagrada, as the inscriptions on the towers themselves say, Gaudí wanted to sing a loud "hosannah in excelsis" (the letters descending on individual shields) to the God his temple so explicitly praises. The bishop's panoply of crozier and mitre is fairly obvious, as are the rosaries garlanded around both pinnacles. Less obvious are the vegetable shapes on some of the lower towers. On closer inspection, these reveal themselves as heads of cereal grasses, including wheat, which have been interpreted as symbolising the heights of religious aspiration. They may also carry references to the staff of life and, a constant in Gaudí's extensive library of symbols, the spiritual benefit to be found in hard work and productivity.

The psychedelic Christmas trees that materialise at points around the building are not as easy to decode, nor are the asymmetrical *trencadis* designs, which at the time of their construction unwittingly echoed the lines, angles and colors of the cubist movement as it invaded galleries across Europe. (Gaudí walked out of a cubist exhibition, dismissing it as "nothing.") Nor can we find any conventional explanation for the strange coronas of spheres decorating the crosses at the top of the pinnacles. These multicolored accretions of melon-like globes could represent fruit and fecundity.

However, given that Gaudí employed virtually identical colored forms for the fantastical roof garden of the Palau Güell, it is possible that another, secular (perhaps Catalanist or Jocs Florals) agenda is at work in these glorious bursts of light and color. Since no definite proof has been left (or at least discovered) it is impossible to tell. As with so much of Gaudí's life and work there will always be unanswered questions of his intent, faith and even devotion. Which is partly why he remains such a fascinating and involving man. Few architects of the 19th century are remembered or held in such high regard as this contradictary and complex Catalan.

EL TEMPLO EXPIATORIO DE LA SAGRADA FAMILIA

THE FINAL JUDGEMENT

Courtesy of Richard Bryant/Arcaid

ALTHOUGH it is nowadays almost wholly given over to a museum (and Gaudí's own Sarcophagus, visible at a lower level through a glass aperture), the crypt was originally where Gaudí figured death and the fate of mankind. This endgame in the cycle he planned for the temple actually starts outside, in the Nativity façade (right), where a group of trumpeting angels is calling mankind to the Final Judgement. The Final Judgement itself is symbolized by a throne in the crypt from which the Almighty will judge mankind. Hell is represented in the vaults at the Carrer Mallorca end of the crypt. Glory, and redemption, are represented outside the church again, in a flock of choiring angels.

As Joan Bergós points out, the scheme represents a comprehensive history of mankind, or indeed creation; from the beginning of time until its end. Gaudí also intended a further, final touch that has yet to be added. After this roller-coaster ride through Creation, the Fall, Judgement, Redemption and Glory, the weary believer would encounter purification in a 20-foot-high jet fountain, falling into a basin of four shells arranged around a representation of the Lamb of God.

Although the average observer could be forgiven for missing this symbolic program, it is the promise of redemption that Gaudí and his friends on the Christian right wanted their expiatory temple to offer the people of the city. History, and the people of Barcelona, would prove less than grateful, however, not least during the Civil War, when angry crowds torched parts of the temple. As with so much of the Sagrada there is an uneasy contradiction and horrible irony in the fact that today the area dedicated to death sees more life than any other.

EL TEMPLO EXPIATORIO DE
LA SAGRADA FAMILIA

SAGRADA FAMILIA PARISH
SCHOOL

Courtesy of the Institut Amatller d'Art Hispánic

TODAY the small schoolhouse to the right of the Passion façade is the only remaining indicator of a comprehensive social program that Gaudí intended the temple to establish. If his camouflaged "cathedral" was to become a beacon and focus for a revival in spirituality, it needed to involve itself in the material world of the community it served, or perhaps dominated. As well as hosting educational and social events, Gaudí saw that the temple would need to integrate itself into the everyday life of its congregation.

The only physical example of this program to be completed was the small schoolhouse in the grounds of the temple. Constructed in 1909–10, the building departs entirely from the plans for the Sagrada Familia and harks back to two earlier Gaudí projects. Most notably, the undulating wave form of the roof echoes the wave in the walls of the Finca Miralles of 1901–2. Gaudí elaborated on the Miralles wall, however, by having the waves flowing in cross-rhythms across the roof. The effect, from either side, is of a further wave peak seen behind the trough of the nearer of the two. Gaudí also upended the wave and sent it rippling around the exterior wall of the building, creating an organic shape not unlike that of the floor plan of the Casa Milà. It is a minor work, wholly overshadowed by the temple, but like the Park Güell lodges, it is an exquisite miniature.

El Templo Expiatorio de la Sagrada Familia

Sagrada Familia parish school

Courtesy of the Institut Amatller d'Art Hispánic

THE Sagrada Familia school may in fact prove to be the one project that fulfilled the didactic function that Gaudí built into so many of his projects. Moreover, it opened, completed, and without any recriminations between architect and owner. Gaudí even managed to install a small sculpture of Sant Jordi, St George, over the door, the better, he said, to educate the pupils about their city and state patron saint, Jordi.

Today, the Sagrada Familia parish school is one of the areas off-limits to visitors, and is currently used as a workspace for the continuing construction work on the temple. A neighboring building also deserves mention, not least for its links to the temple, its designer and the educational work of the school. When Gaudí abandoned his home in the Park Güell to live in the grounds of the Sagrada Familia, he built his *obrador*, studio or atelier, next to the school. Like the parish school, this too departed the plan for the temple with a radical flourish that invites comparison with Frank Gehry's breathtaking Guggenheim Museum in Bilbao. The *obrador*, which served as both studio and college for a small group of Gaudí's architectural students, was, like the parish school, another exquisite miniature of unintentional avant-gardism. The waves from the parish school roof were here heaped up into a wild storm swell. Small minaret towers burst from four-square corners surmounted by fanciful arches. Miradors gave on to ski-slope roofs above glass-walled studio spaces. Windows resembled caves, and in the middle sat something resembling a futuristic butter dish. The *obrador* was burnt to the ground during the Civil War, but, like its parent, the temple, it is gradually being rebuilt.

GLOSSARY

Archivolt A molding, plain or decorated, around the interior surface of an arch.

Art Nouveau School of French decorative artists from the 1890s, taking influence from sinuous shapes in plants and nature.

Basilica Rectangular church plan, of medieval origin, with naves, apses, and aisles.

Casa pairal Catalan term for family (usually rural) home. Also symbolic of the Catalan family, and Catalan identity and culture.

Castellation Castle-like features (battlements, spires, towers etc.), specifically when used as an anachronistic architectural feature.

Catalanism Cultural and political movement that coalesced in the mid-19th century promoting Catalan language, culture, and identity.

Catenary arch Arch formed by the line a string or other free-hanging material forms when strung between two points, such as a ceiling and a column.

Chamfer Any corner where the apex or point has been cut at 45 degrees.

Constructivism Russian avant-garde art movement of the 1920s devoted to three-dimensional representations of cubist techniques. Also noted for the work of figures such as Mayakovsky and El Lissitsky as well as sculptors including Naum Gabo and Britain's Barbara Hepworth. Gaudí is seen as an early influence on the school.

Corbel Protruding support, like a bracket, often of stone or brick, supporting an upper level or feature.

Crenellations Patterned square indentations, such as battlements.

Dada Provocative nihilist art movement formed in 1916 by Hans Arp, Hugo Ball, and Tristan Tzara, promoting anarchy, nonsense, and "readymade" art using found objects (such as Marcel Duchamp's urinal *Fountain*).

Doric column Classic Greek column, with no base, a fluted shaft, and a square form on top.

Eixample The "extension" of old Barcelona, beyond its former city walls, in a grid-like shape to the north-west of the city which would feature many of Gaudí's major projects.

Espantabrujera From the Spanish "espantar" (scare) and "bruja" (witch), literally a "witch-scarer," a chimneypiece molded into a head-like shape to prevent witches from landing on the roof of a house, commonly found in provincial communities.

Futurism Art movement founded by Italian poet Filippo Tommaso Marinetti in his first *Futurist Manifesto* (1909), hymning warfare, automotive speed, and the kinetic angles and lines of machinery.

Gable Either the triangular part of an end-wall below the twin slopes of a pitched (sloping) roof, or a vertical ornamental shape where roof meets façade.

Gothic Style of architecture from northern Europe during the 12th to 16th centuries, typically featuring flying buttresses and vaulted ceilings.

Helical column Column with a square base that twines upwards into a seemingly cylindrical spiral, or helix.

Hypostyle Any structure in which the roof is supported by columns.

Impressionism French art movement christened in the 1870s and typified by Monet, Renoir, and others. The impressionists sought to represent landscape as a glimpse or "impression" in atmospheric light conditions.

Jocs Florals Poetry and arts festival (English: Floral Games) first staged in the 14th century and linked to the medieval Troubadour poets. Died out in the 16th century but was launched anew in the 1850s, as a vehicle for Catalanist culture.

Keystone The central stone in an arch, ceiling or dome.

Llar de foc Inglenook family hearth (typically in a rural "casa pairal": see above) seen as the central symbol of the equally symbolic Catalan home.

Marian Adjective pertaining to the cult of adoration for the Virgin Mary.

Medievalism Styles from the pre-Renaissance period between the 5th and 15th centuries, or the modern use of styles from the period.

Modernisme/modernista: Noun and adjective for the "modernist" school that flourished in Barcelona between the 1870s and 1910s, inspired by the French art nouveau and German *Jugendstil* schools. Gaudí is often mistakenly included in their number. A more typical modernista would be Lluis Domenech i Montaner.

Mudéjar Distinct from "Moorish," *Mudéjar* denotes a Moorish-influenced form of Spanish architecture, dating from the centuries prior to the Christian Reconquest (1080–1492) but popular among modernista architects and designers.

Nave The central space of a church, commonly the rectangular space between door and altar.

Oriel A bay window, often ornamented and supported by corbels.

Parabolic arch An arch defined by a vertical conic form intersected by an imaginary plane parallel to its side, such as the Palau Güell entrance.

Portico Covered entrance or porch.

Proto-modernist Exhibiting modernist influences without claiming them.

Ruralism British school of design from the late 19th century that promoted an idealized form of rustic craftsmanship.

Setmana Trágica Workers' uprising in February 1909 that spilled over into violence against the Catholic church, which was seen as complicit with the government.

Talaiot Prehistoric stone structures found in the countryside of Mallorca and Menorca.

Torre Tower. In Catalan "torre" is also colloquial for a second home, usually in the countryside.

Trefoil Shape in the form of three leaves.

Trencadis mosaic From the Catalan verb "trencar," to break—a mosaic made from deliberately (rather than accidentally) broken materials. Robert Hughes, among other critics, credits Gaudí with "inventing" the collage technique.

Transverse cross Literally "cross-wise," a cross with four rather than two horizontal bars, projecting at 90 degree angles to each other.

Vorticism Avant-garde art movement founded in Britain during 1914 by the writer and painter Wyndham Lewis, borrowing techniques from cubism and futurism to reflect the kinetic "vortices" (spirals or whirlpools) of modern life.

Witch-scarers *see* espantabrujeras.

FURTHER READING

Bassegoda i Nonell, Joan *La Pedrera de Gaudí*
   (Fundació Caixa de Catalunya, 1989).
Bassegoda i Nonell, Joan *Antonio Gaudí, Master Architect* (Abbeville Press, 2000).
Bergós i Massó, Joan *Gaudí, the Man and His Work* (Bullfinch Press, 1999).
Carandell, Josep M & Pere Vivas *Park Güell, Gaudí's Utopia*
   (Triangle Postals, 1998).
Carandell, Josep M & Pere Vivas *El Templo de la Sagrada Familia*
   (Triangle Postals, 1997).
Collins, George *Antoni Gaudí* (Braziller Editions, 1960).
Gómez Serrano, Josep *L'obrador de Gaudí*
   (Edicions UPC, Universitat Politecnica de Catalunya, 1996).
Guell, Xavier *Antoni Gaudí, Obras y Proyectos* (Editorial Gustavo Gili, 1997).
Kent, Conrad and Prindle, Dennis *Park Güell*
   (Princeton Architectural Press, 1993).
de Solà-Morales, Ignasi *Fin de Siècle Architecture in Barcelona*
   (Editorial Gustavo Gili, 1992).
Zerbst, Rainer *Antoni Gaudí* (Taschen, 1985).

GAUDÍ WEBSITES

Gaudí Club: Club for Gaudí aficionados, with images, merchandise, conferences, and organized tours:
http://www.gaudiclub.com/

Sagrada Familia official website: Website devoted to the Sagrada Familia:
http://www.sagradafamilia.org/

Ciutat Gaudí: Gallery of Gaudí images
http://www.geocities.com/SoHo/7745/

Gaudí Central: Private website dedicated to Gaudí's work
http://www.op.net/~jmeltzer/gaudi.html